Dialogue in the Di

C000263606

Combining literary criticism and theory with anthropology and cognitive science, this highly relevant book argues that we are fundamentally shaped by dialogue. Patrick Grant looks at the manner in which dialogue informs and connects the personal, political, and religious dimensions of human experience and how literacy is being eroded through many factors, including advances in digital technology.

The book begins by tracing the history of evolved communication skills and looks at ways in which interconnections among tragedy, the limits of language, and the silence of abjection contribute to an adequate understanding of dialogue. Looking at examples such as "truth decay" in journalism and falling literacy levels in school, alongside literary texts from Malory and Shakespeare, Grant shows how literature and criticism embody the essential values of dialogue. The maintenance of complex reading and interpretive skills is recommended for the recuperation of dialogue and for a better understanding of its fundamental significance in the shaping of our personal and social lives.

Tapping into debates about the value of literature and the humanities, and the challenges posed by digitalization, this book will be of interest and significance to people working in a wide range of subjects, including literary studies, communication studies, digital humanities, social policy, and anthropology.

Patrick Grant is professor emeritus at the University of Victoria, British Columbia, Canada.

Dialogue in the Digital Age

Why it Matters How We Read and What We Say

Patrick Grant

 Routledge
Taylor & Francis Group

LONDON AND NEW YORK

First published 2021
by Routledge
2 Park Square, Milton Park, Abingdon, Oxon OX14 4RN

and by Routledge
605 Third Avenue, New York, NY 10017

Routledge is an imprint of the Taylor & Francis Group, an informa business

British Library Cataloguing-in-Publication Data
A catalogue record for this book is available from the British Library

Library of Congress Cataloging-in-Publication Data
Names: Grant, Patrick, 1941- author.
Title: Dialogue in the digital age : why it matters how we read and what we say / Patrick Grant.
Description: London ; New York : Routledge, 2020. | Series: Routledge focus on literature | Includes bibliographical references and index.
Identifiers: LCCN 2020037479 (print) | LCCN 2020037480 (ebook) | ISBN 9780367688066 (hardback) | ISBN 9781003139812 (ebook)
Subjects: LCSH: Dialogue--Philosophy. | Dialogues--Social aspects. | Literature--History and criticism. | Criticism.
Classification: LCC P95.455 .G73 2020 (print) | LCC P95.455 (ebook) | DDC 801/.3--dc23
LC record available at https://lccn.loc.gov/2020037479
LC ebook record available at https://lccn.loc.gov/2020037480

ISBN 13: 978-0-367-68806-6 (hbk)

Typeset in Times New Roman
by MPS Limited, Dehradun

To Peter Stoepker

The highest activity a human being
can attain is learning for understanding,
because to understand is to be free.

Baruch Spinoza

And life cannot submit itself to reason,
because the end of life is
living and not understanding.

Miguel de Unamuno

Contents

Foreword

Initially, I had thought to write about the value of literary studies for the development of critical thinking and the maintenance of high standards of written communication. Partly in light of recent, rapid advances in information technology, I then shifted my attention to dialogue, a change of focus that allowed me some broader scope to assess how we communicate with each other in civil and political life at a time when standards of literacy and civil discourse are suffering widespread erosion. Throughout, I maintain that literature and criticism are fundamentally dialogical, and so my original interest in these topics remains central to the discussion.

In looking back to the pre-literate phases of human communication and for an account of the evolution of our linguistic skills, I draw especially on the groundbreaking studies of Robert N. Bellah and Merlin Donald. In the assessment of dialogue, and to explain how art is dialogical, I draw especially on Hans-Georg Gadamer and Mikhail Bakhtin. For a prospective view (including relations among dialogue, tragedy, and the political order), I draw especially on Karl Jaspers, Jacques Derrida, and Jacques Lacan. I refer also to a number of studies in which I have attempted to take account of relationships between the idea of culture and the meaning of persons, the impact of the Scientific Revolution on literary discourse, and the claims of the perennial philosophy. Several positions worked out in these enquiries enable the present book to make its case more clearly and, I hope, effectively. In brief, this case is that we are fundamentally shaped by dialogue, of which art is a symbol and efficacious means, and our personal and political lives are adversely affected when literacy is eroded and dialogical discourse prevented or impoverished.

Acknowledgments

With thanks, yet again, to Sue Mitchell. Thanks also to Terry Humby, Hans Luijten, and Henry Summerfield, who have listened patiently and responded thoughtfully throughout. And thanks to Peter Stoepker, who has taught me so much about language.

1 Why dialogue? A brief introduction

Discussions about dialogue take us a long way back – at least to Plato, whose magisterial reflections on the topic some 2,500 years ago are a "shoreless sea",[1] as Robert N. Bellah says, that through the ages has attracted a vast flotilla of further adventurers and explorers.

Central to Plato's view of dialogue is the idea that people learn how to think and to re-evaluate their most deeply held ideas and convictions by entering into discussion with one another in a co-operative, if also mutually challenging, spirit. This spirit is acquired by practice and is marked by a willingness to participate in the process of discovering where a particular line of enquiry might lead. The personalities of the participants are part of this process because the feeling-structures that underlie and inform thinking also help to shape people's moral, aesthetic, and religious evaluations and commitments. In short, dialogical thinking is embodied, and is not limited to an exchange of abstract ideas; rather, in dialogue thinking remains complex and open-ended just as persons also are open-ended, always unfinished.

Most discussions of dialogue, as well as most written dialogues, return more or less to these core concerns. This book is no exception, and throughout, following Plato, I emphasize that the dialogical and the personal are closely interconnected. I do so in response especially to the prevailing climate of the times today, in which a virtual sacralizing of the individual is accompanied by an equivalent diminishment of the idea of the person, so that the differences between individuals and persons are hardly noticed at all. The political implications of those differences are therefore also likewise largely ignored.

Not-so-free enterprise

From its beginnings – roughly, let us say, with the decline of feudalism – the free-enterprise system has depended on the versatility and dynamism of the markets to channel the flow of capital, and on the state to protect the markets from criminal interference and unfair practices. As Robert Heilbroner says, "there has never been such a social mechanism for sustained economic progress", and yet throughout its history the free-enterprise system – or capitalism – has generated "wealth and misery simultaneously". That is, at every phase capitalism has brought about new forms of suffering and deprivation as a side effect of its success. Because the logic of the markets is, as Heilbroner says, "as impersonal as that of military tactics",[2] the dehumanizing consequences of this "mechanism" for progress are often written off more or less as collateral damage. Plenty of conscionable people, of course, have attended – and go on attending – philanthropically to the casualties of the system that they nonetheless simultaneously perpetuate. But however admirable, the goodwill of private individuals has hardly been sufficient to offset a great many widespread and often cruel inequalities as well as a great deal of avoidable suffering.

Political processes in many countries have indeed done much to correct at least some of the worst depredations of capitalist excess – through labor laws, public health, social security, and so on. And yet, on a massive scale, transnational capital today continues to outreach the political checks that would modify the indifference with which profits continue to be put before people. Also, with the morphing of industrial capital into financial capital, new crises have arisen from within the system and continue to be absorbed by it. As always, the main driver of the process at large, whether on the expanding out-of-control perimeter or at the established, unassailable center, is self-interest, the law of each against all in the drive to get ahead. Under such conditions, it is entirely understandable that a high value should be placed on the idea of individual freedom, even though, as a moment's reflection confirms, within such a dispensation people are not so much free as isolated, insofar as each is in competition with all the others. The market might well be free, but the "individuals" who are hard at work within it are a great deal less self-determining than they often think.

A climate of the times

Ironically, in the present cultural phase the atomizing of individuals and the depersonalizing mechanisms that bring it about are greatly heightened by the communication technologies so remarkably developed by the digital revolution. Cell phones, text messages, Facebook, Twitter, Instagram, emails, and the World Wide Web enable a hyper-communication that all too often turns out to be barely communication at all. One problem is simply that tsunamis of information without context have a fragmenting effect that makes it difficult to develop any patiently consolidated store of personal knowledge from which coherent discourse can be shaped. Even for the many people who bring to bear a developed critical perspective, the task of sifting through the sheer volume of information (and misinformation) is prohibitively taxing and time consuming. Consequently, it is not hard to notice today how a widespread skepticism about public discourse is accompanied by a privileging of emotion over reason – the Like button, as it were – accompanied by a readiness to disregard evidence and reasoned argument. It is hardly surprising that a recent RAND report describes a steady "truth decay" in journalism in the United States during the past three decades as news coverage has shifted increasingly "to opinion-based content that appeals to emotion", while "extreme sources play on people's worst instincts, like fear and tribalism".[3] In addition, a rapid increase in mass surveillance, the widespread political and commercial deployment of algorithms developed by Big Data, the use of "persuasive design" technologies, and targeted advertising are producing the exact opposite of the individual self-determination and freedom that these various thriving enterprises claim to champion.

To make matters more challenging, literacy rates in the United States and Canada today are a cause for serious concern. In the United States, almost one third of the population is "illiterate or barely literate", and approximately 50 percent of adults "can't read a book written at eighth-grade level". In Canada, some 43 percent of adults have low literacy skills – that is, "too low to be fully competent in most jobs in our modern economy". A report from the Organization for Economic Cooperation and Development (2012) assessed literacy among 16- to 19-year-olds in 23 countries. The United Kingdom was in 23rd place, the United States 21st, and Canada 17th.[4] Maryanne Wolf, who writes well about the effects of digital technology on children's learning, reports that "a full two-thirds of U.S. children in the fourth grade do not read at a 'proficient' level". She presents evidence that children who are allowed a lot of screen time do not read, analyze, or comprehend as well as children whose screen time is restricted. Although good reading skills are necessary to "maintain the intellectual, social, and economic health of our country", at the moment "two-thirds or more of future U.S. citizens are not even close".[5] Wolf does not recommend trying, somehow, to turn back the clock. Rather, we should focus on developing biliterate skills, so that the patient work of learning to read, think, and communicate is not neglected, even as more of people's time is taken up by the different kind of attention cultivated by digital communication.

In view of all this, my main point is simple enough: the domain of the abbreviated text message, the Facebook outrage, the 140-character public-policy statement, together with the general, enervating confusion caused by information overload and what the TV commentator Van Jones felicitously calls "cancel culture; call-out culture"[6] (by which he means, I take it, the fashionable strategy of immediate hostile rejection of a dissenting point of view followed immediately by accusation), is not at all what I take dialogue to be. Also, although these indicators of malaise are specific to the present times, it is worth noticing that they reproduce – even as they intensify – the basic alienations caused by a system that from the start has fetishized self-interest and individualism at the expense of the personal. Here, I take "personal" in a quite traditional sense to indicate a way of understanding human beings and the cultural and political means by which they organize their common life. That is, individuals are said to enter into personhood through relationship, entailing a recognition in the other of a sentience and intentionality akin to one's own, together with a shared sense of strangeness, or difference. Because the personal develops always from and through the interpersonal, it follows that in the social sphere the good of all is returned as the good of each, so that the realization of communal goals is also the self-creation of those agents, or persons, who bring them about.[7] The analogue of this process in the realm of verbal discourse is what I mean by dialogue.

Embodied mosaic

The analogy between dialogue and the personal remains at the heart of what I want to say in the following pages. Also, I want to suggest that in dialogue the full range of human language comes into play, so that language is not confined to its depersonalizing, instrumental uses. Rapid symbolic speech, which is unique to *Homo sapiens*, is an immensely powerful evolutionary advantage, but it is also a mosaic of discrete structures and skills. As the evolutionary principle of the conservation of gains reminds us, new skills build on and incorporate earlier ones, so that a breakdown at an underlying level will disrupt whatever more specialized abilities develop afterwards. It is likely that the earliest underpinnings of human speech were in what Darwin calls "rudimentary song" – that is, cries and signals presumably expressing fear, pain, triumph, alarm, and so on. Over time, further layers of communication were added through aggregation and syntheses to produce a complex network, not always without internal frictions. As Merlin Donald shows in detail, bodily gestures developed toward mimetic displays and, with the advent of spoken language, into storytelling, dance, and ritual.[8] The eventual development of second-order thinking (reflection on the process itself of thinking), and the advent of writing and printing, rapidly increased the power of language and brought about a radical reorganization of human society. Today, digital communication technologies are developing at such speed that a major challenge is to understand how the entire computational turn belongs within the story as a whole and how to manage it while remaining mindful of the earlier strata that continue to underpin and sustain it.

It is not always easy to be mindful, however. A stock-market entrepreneur might all too readily ignore the stories and traditions underpinning a way of life in a local community that happens to present an investment opportunity. Likewise, the deliberate appropriation and manipulation of traditional narratives for merely instrumental purposes, such as the promotion of consumerism or political advantage, might all too readily ignore how ancient myths, stories, and ritual practices can connect people to the basic structures of their coexistence within nature in relation to each other. In turn, this coexistence depends on a pre-articulate recognition and respect (as Emmanuel Levinas strongly argues) that come about through personal, face-to-face meetings, and that cannot escape being undervalued by a culture that excessively promotes individualism and the instrumental uses of language. Instrumental and expedient modes of communication are of course useful – indeed, necessary – for practical purposes. But dialogue is based on an understanding (whether tacit or not) that a habitual curtailment of the full range of our language skills cuts us off from some significant aspect of what constitutes us as persons.

Art as dialogue

But how are we to deal with the fact that dialogue is usually considered to be oral, whereas our civilization has long since come to depend heavily on literacy? One answer is (as Walter Ong shows)[9] that orality and literacy are interwoven, so that in a literate society, dialogue is inseparable from what is learned by reading. Plato was already struggling with this complexity. In the *Phaedrus* (275a), Socrates laments the fact that young people who focus too much on reading will be less able to remember well and, consequently, will be less able to participate in dialogue, which is oral. But throughout the *Laws* (from which Socrates is absent), a great many regulations are described as set down in writing because society cannot go on depending solely on oral tradition. This tension between the claims of orality and literacy is reproduced throughout the *Dialogues*, in which Socrates performs orally but is also a character in a literary work. In short, throughout the *Dialogues* oral discourse is written for readers, and if this were not the case, we could not understand the value that Plato attaches to dialogue in the first place. That is, his writing enables him to assess the oral from a critical point of view and attach a value to it. In so doing, he well knew that part of the price to be paid for the advantages of writing is that writing removes us from direct personal encounter with an interlocutor. Plato's insistence on the true spirit of dialogue is therefore itself a warning against the depersonalizing aspects of the written word and, by extension, of concepts divorced from lived experience. Consequently, he takes care to compose the *Dialogues* as dramatized performances inhabited by a range of characters whose personalities shape the discussion, which in turn incorporates poetry, myth, metaphor, symbol, narrative, and literary allusions of many kinds, as well as the dialectic cut and thrust of argument. For Plato, the written word therefore re-creates an experience of oral discourse through the one mode of writing that is best ordered to do this, which is, broadly, what we now refer to as literature. The *Dialogues* do not fall into the chilly impersonality that Plato warns against because, through his literary art, they engage us as readers much as the participants within the dialogue itself are engaged with one another.

The ways in which art and literature are dialogical are explored by, among others, Hans-Georg Gadamer and Mikhail Bakhtin, and the continuity they describe between the dialogical in art and in actual face-to-face exchange remains central to what I want to say in the following pages. And yet it is also the case that art and life are distinct. A painting of a person is not the actual person, and the audience at a tragic drama knows that the protagonist does not really die on stage. In much the same way, we know that burning a book and burning the author are crimes of a different order. That is, although art engages us dialogically, it also creates its own world, distinct from the face-to-face meetings that constitute the dialogical in our actual encounters with others. Nonetheless, we are to remember that art also connects us to the common world of our personal and social relationships. That is, books teach us how to live, and for humans, the art of living, we might say, is also the art of dialogue. Consequently, in a written discussion such as this one, examples from literature are especially helpful in showing how dialogue works. It is as if the dialogue of art is at once a mimesis and a touchstone for the art of dialogue.

What dialogue is (for now)

What, then, do I take dialogue to be? In a sentence, it is *the open-ended process of people thinking creatively together, in which each discovers and decides how to respond by listening to the other*. Dialogue is *open-ended* not least because the mosaic of language reaches back into the body that we do not completely know, just as we do not completely know the other who addresses us. The participants in dialogue think *creatively* because the intent is not to prove a point or win an individual victory, but to find something new and of value by means of what goes between during an interpersonal exchange. Each participant *discovers and decides* what to say because the way forward is uncharted, even as the participants take the steering into their own hands, directed by whatever store of knowledge they already have. Also, dialogue depends on *listening*, which requires holding the ego in abeyance in order to provide accessibility for and to the other, without which dialogue cannot begin. Dialogue then is a response to the other made possible by listening.

The following chapters develop the main points set out in these introductory remarks. Chapter 2 deals with the embodied mosaic of language and with the interplay within language between conservation and open-endedness. Chapter 3 deals with the primacy of listening and with the interplay between participation and misrecognition in the imperfect process of thinking together, in which something new might be discovered. Chapter 4 deals with the limits of dialogue, and with the challenge presented by tragedy, which beggars language. Chapter 5 deals with the encounter between decision-making and aporia in negotiating an uncharted way forward through the dialogical process.

As far as the book as a whole is concerned, the wind behind its sails, as I began by saying, blows from a long way back. One conviction it carries forward is that the patiently acquired values of a humane education should at the very least be an antidote to the depersonalizing excesses of the prevailing climate of the times. Another is that it is worthwhile attempting to articulate the possibility of a participatory, un-self-seeking manner of proceeding with our personal and social lives – a possibility of which dialogue is both a symbol and harbinger.

Notes

1　Robert N. Bellah, *Religion in Human Evolution. From the Paleolithic to the Axial Age* (Cambridge, Massachusetts: Harvard University Press, 2011), p. 38.
2　Robert Heilbroner, *Twenty-First Century Capitalism* (Ontario: Anansi Press, 1992), pp. 40, 43.
3　Marketwatch.com. Quentin Fottrell, May 28, 2019.
4　In general, literacy is assessed across several levels of proficiency, with reference to different groups of people, and is measured on different scales. Much information is available, and it can be confusing, but the overall findings are remarkably consistent. In order of citation, my sources are as follows: Chris Hedges, *Empire of Illusion. The End of Literacy and the Triumph of Spectacle* (Toronto: Alfred K. Knopf, 2009), p. 44; Valerie Strauss, "Hiding in Plain Sight: The Adult Literacy Crisis", *The Washington Post*, November 1, 2016; Arti Patel, "When it Comes to High Literacy, Numeracy Rates, Canada Is Low on the List: Report", *HuffPost* November 1, 2016, updated, May 18, 2017; "Adult Literacy Rate – Low level Skills", The Conference Board of Canada, 2013; Organization for Economic Cooperation and Development (OECD), 2012.
5　Maryanne Wolf, *Reader Come Home: The Reading Brain in a Digital World* (New York: Harper Collins, 2018), pp. 151, 152.
6　On HBO, *Real Time with Bill Maher,* Friday, May 10, 2019.
7　I have written further about the idea of the person, for example in *Personalism and the Politics of Culture* (London: Macmillan, 1996).
8　Merlin Donald, *Origins of the Modern Mind. Three Stages in the Evolution of Culture and Cognition* (Cambridge, Massachusetts: Harvard University Press, 1991). I deal with this book in more detail in Chapter 2.
9　See, for example, *Orality and Literacy: The Technologizing of the Word.* 2nd ed. (New York: Routledge, 2002).

2 A manner of speaking

Two minutes to midnight

Since 1947, a group of scientists has been adjusting the Doomsday Clock to indicate how close the world is to destruction caused by technologies of our own invention. In 2018, the big hand was nudged ahead to two minutes to midnight – closer by 30 seconds than the year before, and as close as it has been since 1953, when the United States and Russia tested their first thermonuclear weapons. To a surprising degree, the written report on the 2018 assessment is preoccupied with language. Among other things, it singles out the negative effects on democracy and world peace of "hyperbolic rhetoric", unclear and unreliable political pronouncements, the reduction of diplomacy to "name-calling", and the confusions caused by widespread disinformation. It seems that a failure or debasement of language, especially among those in positions of public responsibility, has played a significant role in bringing us as close to midnight as we have ever been.[1]

But then, perhaps the scientists are overstating the case. Don't their own words come suspiciously close to the hyperbolic rhetoric that they condemn? And isn't there a touch of Disneyland villainy, after all, in that slightly cartoonish notion of a Doomsday Clock? Besides, don't the scientists have a political agenda of their own that influences their opinions?

In shifting the focus as I have just done in the previous paragraph, from the truth claims of the Doomsday statement to the credibility of the authors, I am resorting to an old strategy that in recent decades has come so vigorously into its own as to seem now almost normal. That is, attacking the messenger seems preferable to giving due consideration to the message. Today, the excess of rapidly available information together with an immediate, engulfing overgrowth of reactions to it feeds into an exponentially expanding universe of discourse within which it is often difficult to find one's bearings. Consequently, it is inviting to respond to information almost as if it is an advertisement for a product that you might or might not be attracted to buy, depending on your tastes and preferences. It is easy then to feel an imagined solidarity with others who are like-minded insofar as their tastes and preferences resemble your own. By contrast, information you don't happen to find agreeable is not so much explored as rejected as false advertising or discredited, for instance as "fake news", because of the imputed motivations of the (unlikeable) people – the messengers – who gave voice to the opinions in the first place.

One fairly obvious problem with this largely affect-based, partisan strategy for dealing with today's rapid oversupply of information is that it so effectively short-circuits discussion. By and large, there is not enough time to sort matters out and to shape judgements based on respect for evidence, careful reasoning, and a willingness to listen to opposing points of view or to discuss problems by way of direct personal exchange with others who have informed opinions about the matter at hand. In a prescient sentence written in 1951, Martin Buber states, "If we ever reach the stage of making ourselves understood only by means of the dictograph, that is, without contact with one another, the chance of human growth would be indefinitely lost".[2] Buber was not imagining the internet or the iPad or the smartphone ("dictograph" now sounds quaint), but it would have come as no surprise to him that today a variety of educators, linguists, psychologists, and neurologists are finding that overexposure to digital communication and to the information overload that comes along with it is adversely affecting not only the reading comprehension and analytical skills of high school and university students but also their capacity for empathy. As Maryanne Wolf says, our "highly elaborated reading brain" operates through a set of processes that enable "internalized knowledge, analytical reasoning, and inference; perspective-taking and empathy; critical analysis and the generation of insight". But a "subtle atrophy" of these abilities has become a matter of concern in a world deluged as never before by inflammatory, often contradictory information which, if unchecked and unanalyzed, leaves us susceptible, among other things, to "demagoguery". Also, the fact that the atrophy Wolf describes is not confined to reading comprehension but extends to empathy means that it reaches to the very core of our capacity for humane relationships. She points to an ominously precipitous decline in empathy among young people in the United States during the past two decades, which she sees as a source of "unwitting ignorance, fear and misunderstanding" that in turn can lead to "belligerent forms of intolerance".[3] And so it seems that impoverished language, diminished critical ability, and a stunting of empathy reinforce one another, and the social and political consequences are troubling. As Buber says, in such circumstances the opportunity for human growth itself is undermined, and certainly today the rush to spectral, disembodied modes of communication is all too effectively separating and isolating individuals even while offering to connect them. Little wonder, then, with so much that is divided, disenchanted, and at the same time desperate for attention, that there should be a widespread recoil of cynicism and frustration, and that a groundswell of populist reaction, especially in North America and Europe, should be turning now, inchoate, in a slow vortex of resentment. Increasingly, its allegiances are tribal, driven by affect, as it feeds the rough beasts of blood-and-soil nationalism and demagoguery. This too is part of the climate of the times.

Not surprisingly, in such circumstances specialized expertise is often also regarded with suspicion. Here it is helpful to return to the Doomsday Clock and to the words of Rachel Bronson, who writes that in addition to what the 2018 report says, we need to be concerned about "increasing attacks on experts and expertise world wide at the exact moment when such expertise is needed".[4] That is, the hyperbolic rhetoric, name-calling, and the plague of misinformation mentioned in the 2018 report have produced a general atmosphere of cynicism that spills over into a lack of respect for expertise in general. All too often, little acknowledgment is given to the fact that expert knowledge is the result of patient study, co-operative learning, and well-tried practice, and is acquired by people who value such unglamorous processes as peer assessment and maintaining high standards. Yes, experts can be wrong, and the processes of peer assessment and accreditation are too often flawed, but it is preferable, surely, to have a urologist rather than a plumber perform your bladder surgery, just as it is better to have a plumber rather than a urologist install your hot-water tank. That is easy enough to see, but in a world where confusions among marketing, entertainment, and politics can make it difficult to tell experts from charlatans, it is easy to see also that an exaggerated scapegoating of "experts" in general should afford some sense of relief – some affective respite – from a contagion of frustration and cynicism increasingly expressed as resentment against established authority. But to prejudge from a position driven by affect and confirmed by polarizing allegiances that seek to justify their own oversimplifications by peremptory denunciation is also to preclude the kinds of engagement by means of which creative transformations are effected that alone can make a real and helpful difference. As Buber says, approaches to knowledge that prevent personal communication through dialogue destroy our capacity for growth by ignoring the complexities that make us what we are. And as Wolf shows, part of this complexity is that traditional reading skills remain the indispensable underpinnings of modern culture and need to be preserved, not least because of the analytical abilities and empathetic understandings that they help to cultivate. What prior communication skills, then, underpin our ability to read well? It is a long story, as long a story as there is.

The big picture: the stories we tell

The traditional scriptures, doctrines, and practices of the world's major religions preserve a record of the oldest stories and cultural formations by means of which people have attempted to make sense of the world we so improbably find ourselves inhabiting. Today it is broadly (though not universally) acknowledged that, across the globe, the vast spectrum of religious claims and practices are so interwoven and yet so often incompatible that none of them can any longer make credible claims to hold the truth exclusively. No doubt, plenty of their adherents continue to feel otherwise, but as Charles Taylor writes, naivete about such matters is "now unavailable to anyone, believer or unbeliever alike".[5] And so, in the interests at least of avoiding naivete, it might be a good idea to acknowledge at the start that the over-arching enigmas of birth and death remain just that – nobody knows what happens when we die, or what the meaning of it all is. The teachings of the world's major religions can then best be seen as offering values and guidelines that might help people to negotiate the crises of life while preserving a sense of shared meaning and purpose in relation to the unresolvable conundrum of what we are doing here in the first place. In this broad context, it is helpful to recall that the visionary experiences described by the saints and mystics in every major religious tradition are, as a matter of course, skeptically regarded by the custodians of orthodoxy. This is so not least because the saints and mystics tend to insist on the provisional status of traditional symbols and teachings. They remind us that words and explanations fall short, and the mystery remains as unexplainable as it is immediate.[6] In the 18th century, the unbelieving David Hume astutely remarked that skeptics and mystics are much alike in looking askance at attempts to explain the unexplainable.[7] And so, simply put, there is no complete or final revelation, and the holy books were written after all by human beings within certain historical circumstances, sometimes drawing on preceding oral traditions, sometimes edited and augmented over long periods of time. Likewise, myths of origin develop in the same way. They are collectively held stories offering explanations that provide identity and meaning to the communities that share them, and their symbolic power is often useful in helping people to interpret the world, the better to survive in it. This is not to say that myths, as with every other human invention, cannot be wrenched into forms that serve the interests of the unscrupulous, bent on exploitation and oppression.

Modern evolutionary theory is also a story of origins, but it differs from traditional myths insofar as it is supported by evidence from a broad range of scientific disciplines.[8] Geology, biology, anthropology, comparative anatomy, genetic science, and astronomy, in combination with measurements provided by carbon 14 and argon-argon dating techniques, thermoluminescence, paleomagnetism, biochronology, and the rates of mutation measured by molecular clocks – all this offers a broad, evidence-based consensus, sufficient to command the assent of reasonable people. We should not, therefore, take literally the truth claims of ancient myths of origin when they clash with what this better evidence shows us. For example, the story in Genesis of God creating the world in six days cannot be literally true. The early church fathers already realized this, not least because the word "day" cannot have its current meaning before the creation of the sun, which, according to Genesis, occurred on the fourth day. "Day" must therefore mean a certain phase or period to be understood symbolically, as Augustine, for example, states.[9]

Nonetheless, some hardy literalists go on insisting that the world is some 6,000 to 10,000 years old and that dinosaurs were companions of Adam and Eve. In museums dedicated to the cause, they will show you this, dioramas and all.[10] But it is a nonsense, and it won't do for "creationists" to claim that Genesis offers an account on equal footing with evolutionary theory, as if they are commensurate kinds of explanation. Northrop Frye[11] (who was a Christian) correctly explains that the biblical creation stories are not helpful as literal accounts of the origins of the cosmos. Rather, they are records of the coming to human consciousness of fundamental questions about our existence. What is the meaning of the universe? Where do we stand within it and how is it ordered? What are our responsibilities and limitations? Along similar lines, Robert Alter[12] shows that two main premises underlie the opening chapters of Genesis. The first is that there is an overarching divine order, and the second is that humans are free moral agents. The Bible then goes on to develop a vision of the human condition in response to these foundational moral intuitions in a manner that continues to have a profound shaping effect on a wide range of human cultures.

By contrast to the narrative, poetic, and moral complexities of the Bible, the measurements recorded by molecular clocks are indeed coldly impersonal, even though they give us facts of the matter that we had better not ignore. But we should not find it surprising that scientists can also be religious believers; even though the scientific account of evolution is factual, the overarching enigma endures. The unfathomable outer reaches of the cosmos and the inner depths of consciousness still evoke the wonder and amazement that gave rise to ancient mythology in the first place, and for some people the appeal of a symbolic address to the mystery, such as religion provides, is understandable. And so the wisdom traditions of the major world religions that today are willing to incorporate an intelligent self-understanding in relation to modern science as well as to other belief traditions – including secular unbelief – might well provide a responsibly informed, life-enhancing address to the encompassing challenges of life and death for which there is as yet no instrumental solution and which must be lived through by each of us.

But just as mythology is not an escapist fiction, so it is worth emphasizing also that science is not concerned only with measurement and calculation. At the beginning of the Scientific Revolution, Francis Bacon was keen to remove the contaminations of imagination from scientific experimentation, but philosophers of science have long acknowledged that imagination plays a significant role in scientific discovery.[13] In short, science can be a thing of beauty, just as mythology can be empirically useful. In this context, it is worth remembering that the theory of evolution is constructed as a narrative – a story that no doubt will undergo alterations in light of future discoveries. But as Robert N. Bellah says, this narrative happens to be the only story of origins that is shared globally today by the majority of educated people. This is so because the evidence that it is a true story is so compelling.[14] Nonetheless, as Bellah goes on to show, the major world religions can help us to understand the course of human cultural evolution as a continuing narrative extending from prehistoric myth to modern science, and as Merlin Donald argues, it is not helpful to ignore or neglect the distinctive kinds of knowledge and understanding achieved at any of the key stages of this development. That is, science does not altogether cancel the insights and moral values discovered during the early phases of human development. Rather, many of these insights and values continue to be sustaining and need to be assessed appropriately. By analogy, I want to maintain that dialogue likewise recapitulates this same evolutionary development, as it engages language in the full spectrum of its evolved complexity.

Evolution: beginning again at the beginning

The beginning[15] was some 13.5 billion years ago, and the metaphor enabling us to grapple with the initiating event (yes, the mystery endures) is that there was a Big Bang, an explosion outward into manifestation of matter, time, and space. Within a universe comprising billions upon billions of stars and countless further billions of planets, the earth was formed some 4.5 billion years ago, and during roughly the next billion years, life began. Single cells developed into primitive organisms, and from about 600 million years ago arthropods, fish, plants, amphibians, and reptiles emerged. The age of the dinosaurs lasted for some 160 million years, from about 225 million years ago until about 65 million years ago. The great apes (comprising chimpanzees, gorillas, bonobos, and orangutans) emerged some 14 million years ago, and about 5 million years ago humans diverged from chimpanzees. About 4 million years ago, *Australopithecus* was our first ancestor to live on the savanna. The australopithecines were bipedal and might have used tools, but there is no evidence of these being set aside for repeated use. By contrast, the shadowy figure of *Homo habilis* used tools regularly about 2 million years ago, and the picture becomes a great deal clearer with *Homo erectus*, who developed a distinctive tool kit and also migrated widely out of Africa. *Homo erectus* stayed remarkably stable for almost 2 million years, from about 1.5 million years ago until becoming extinct some 33,000 years ago. But there were also several other species within the genus *Homo*: in addition to *Homo habilis* and *Homo erectus*, others such as *Homo rudolfensis*, *Homo heidelbergensis*, *Homo neanderthalensis*, *Homo denisova*, *Homo ergaster*, and *Homo floresiensis* have been identified, and further proliferations and extinctions might still be discovered. It is unclear how responsible the fast-talking, technologically inventive *Homo sapiens* was for the disappearance of the several other competing *Homo* species, but the fact is that they are extinct.

Sapiens arrived on the scene perhaps 200,000 years ago, and at some time between roughly 150,000 and 50,000 years ago acquired speech, though how this occurred remains unclear. Certainly, from about 50,000 years ago human culture changed rapidly, as is evidenced by complex hunting techniques, ritual burials, and intricately fashioned clothes and ornaments. The sophistication of these achievements suggests that our characteristic rapid symbolic speech was an adjunct to and also a means of enabling them. The great number of languages, myths, and narratives that no doubt proliferated at this time are lost to us because there was no way to record them.

The last ice age ended roughly 10,000 years ago, providing the conditions for agriculture to develop rapidly, if unevenly, with far-reaching effects on human social organization. From some 4 million years ago, our ancestors survived by gathering and hunting, and were organized in small groups that seem to have been more or less egalitarian. But a great deal changed with the Agricultural Revolution, as the domestication of grains and animals provided surpluses that allowed villages to become towns, then cities and empires. Specialized occupations and trades – including, most importantly, the military – enabled the emergence of governing elites, and earlier forms of hunter-gatherer small-group egalitarianism yielded to the authority of all-powerful rulers who were regarded as semidivine and had absolute power over life and death. Subgroups were routinely subjugated or enslaved by the imperium, which nonetheless provided stability within which arts and sciences could flourish. But still, within the new civilized order, the archaic terrors of our remote hunter-gatherer ancestors stayed with us. Those millions of years ago, *Australopithecus* gambled that a bipedal life on the savanna would offer better opportunities for shared parenting and the production of more numerous offspring. But on two legs, unprotected by the trees, they were slow and vulnerable and constantly under threat from powerful predators. Ever watchful and prepared for violence, our hunter-gatherer ancestors in general needed to be constantly prepared for fight or flight. Although towns and cities eventually offered protection from the creatures larger than ourselves lurking in the darkness, the old patterns of response remained. And so, in our meetings with what is strange or different – or might be imagined as threatening or even suspicious – the deep anxieties and aggressions of those remote ancestors flood our amygdalas still, compelling us, often irrationally, toward fear and violence. In addition, enmities within the group, especially over mutually desired objects, can erupt readily into violence, and to this day, intraspecific rivalry remains a main threat to human safety and even survival. The uses of language either to mediate and contain these kinds of rivalries and enmities or to project them onto scapegoats have been studied in detail by anthropologists such as Eric Gans and René Girard.[16]

The advent of civilization also meant that people were employed in specialized occupations, and accounts had to be kept. For that, writing was required, and also money. The earliest cuneiform scripts – so called because they consisted of wedge-shaped incisions on clay tablets – came into use some 5,200 years ago. Initially their scope was limited, but as more signs were added, the range of what the cuneiform tablets could express became broader. Egyptian hieroglyphs developed at roughly the same time, and for the same reasons. Yet both of these forms of writing were difficult and required the use of some 600–700 characters. By contrast, the Phoenician script adapted by the Greeks has given us our 26-letter phonogram system, which can be rapidly learned even by young children and can be used to record an immensely wide range of information. And so reading and civilization developed together, and without writing, the far-reaching Axial Age developments in human thought and speculation could not have brought about the revolution that they did.

The Axial Age (the term was invented by Karl Jaspers)[17] extends roughly from 900 to 200 BCE. Common to the main innovative thinkers of this period, whether in Greece, India, China, or Israel, is the claim that universal ideas and standards should govern human behavior rather than traditional group allegiances and practices rooted in myth and ritual. The Axial Age was therefore revolutionary in bringing to bear critical thought in order to assess the value of traditional myths and narratives and to measure these older forms of thought and communication against the universalizing claims of reason. Not surprisingly, Axial Age philosophers and sages continued to be influenced by the oral traditions that they also challenged, even as they used written language to record the abstract reasoning that their extended critical investigations required. That is, when an argument is stabilized in writing, it can be analyzed and supplemented or corrected accordingly. For instance, in Plato, as in the Buddhist sutras, a fascinating, creative tension runs throughout between the dynamism of orality and the stability of the written text. This same interplay remains very much with us still in day-to-day life, for instance in the competing claims of storytelling and abstract reason, anecdote and analysis, emotional appeal and logical response that we encounter in a wide variety of familiar situations.

Axial Age thinking in the tradition of Plato, with its implicit trust in language to interpret the hierarchical orders of meaning and design that link the heavens and the earth, endured in the West until the period of the Reformation and the Scientific Revolution in the 16th and 17th centuries. The main innovation of the Reformers was to insist on God's transcendence beyond mediation, in order to confirm the core conviction that our immortal souls will not be saved or damned as a result of our own efforts.

Consequently, the mystery of Justification was a central preoccupation of the Reformers, rather than the effort to earn salvation through prayer, good works, and the sacraments of the Church. Meanwhile, the new scientists were also keen to affirm God's transcendence, partly as an expression of piety but also because the relegation of God to the realm of his own mysterious purposes allowed science to get on with investigating the material world according to its particular, immanent laws. Science and Reform therefore enabled a transition from the Axial Age discourse that prevailed through the Middle Ages to modern secularism. In turn, the growing prestige of science and the widespread dismantling of the hierarchies of being that mediate between heaven and earth encouraged the development of highly instrumental attitudes toward the world within which, not surprisingly, capitalism also flourished. Today, the combined forces of technology and capitalism are so powerfully in the ascendant that the complexities of language in expressing the range of human needs and capacities built into our evolutionary history are easily neglected in the interests of efficiency, profit, power, productivity, and the like. But as we also see, today there is a widespread recoil, often expressed as a primitive affective response that in turn can partly be interpreted as a sort of blind repudiation of the ruthlessly depersonalizing compact between technology and global capitalism.

With this broad historical context in mind, I want to argue that dialogue is best understood as effecting a self-conscious recovery of the entire spectrum of language in all its evolved complexity, as a necessary antidote to the debasement and confusions that the Doomsday Clock scientists warn against. And yet, however self-conscious this attempted recovery is, we do not arrive at any point of origin that stands clearly and objectively before us. As Emmanuel Levinas argues,[18] dialogue begins with a response to the other, and the summons that one feels in the approach of another person is an event that can be described only by way of quasi-poetic evocation, because it lies deeper than culture, beyond and before language. It is already present, that is, in the expressiveness of the countenance that makes a moral demand on me even before I can reflect on it. My attention to that presence is therefore a primal acknowledgement of the responsibility by which I am fundamentally constituted as human, and which remains also the tacit foundation of everything subsequently spoken between us. The significance of this event of meeting and recognition cannot be demonstrated from a point of view outside it, but it is the foundation nonetheless of every dialogical exchange.

That tacit foundation – a basic hospitality to the other – is also what Plato points us to in the Seventh Letter[19] when he writes that we cannot have a philosophical discussion with someone who does not enter into the exchange with the right disposition. What Plato is getting at becomes clear in the *Republic*, for instance, when the bullying, egocentric Thrasymachus behaves in such an overbearing manner that there is, as the saying goes, no talking to him. He won't listen, and so the dialogue breaks down. It can resume only when Glaucon and Adeimantus take over, continuing Thrasymachus's arguments but in a different spirit, as they themselves say.[20] The difference lies mainly in their willingness to meet the other participants without rejecting them outright as Thrasymachus had done. Rather, they begin by acknowledging the others as being capable of reflective knowledge and as having a kindred intentionality and feeling. The disposition that Glaucon and Adeimantus bring to the conversation cannot be taught directly, which is one reason why Thrasymachus cannot learn it. It emerges instead from the recognition implicit in our initial, pre-articulate approach to the other, as Levinas says.

Michael Polanyi's[21] entire philosophical vision turns on the closely associated idea that we attend *to* things that we know *from* an antecedent, more complex ground that remains unarticulated but which tacitly supports and enables our ability to focus. We can of course also turn our attention to some aspects of our background assumptions, but in so doing we depend on yet a further "tacit dimension" which in the end eludes our attempts to objectify it because it recedes eventually into the recesses of the body, and then into the body of the world itself and so to the mystery of being that contains all bodies together and that we never know fully. In an analogous way, I want to suggest that in using language we attend from the prior phases of its evolution that continue to underpin our more recently emergent linguistic skills, even though it is not possible to be fully conscious of how this is so, because our meeting and acknowledgement of the other as an interlocutor emerges from a bond of mutual recognition and hospitality that precedes language and therefore remains tacit, as Polanyi shows.

How language got into it

The story of how language developed is widely debated, and in the following account I draw mainly on the sociologist Robert N. Bellah and the psychologist Merlin Donald,[22] both of whom are also highly knowledgeable about anthropology.

Donald invites us to imagine a time when rudimentary vocalizations (cries of alarm, fear, pain, jubilation, and so on) coexisted with gesture as a main means of communication – the prototypes, as it were, of the prosodic (musical) and phonetic (conceptual) aspects of spoken language. But our ability to vocalize well enough to produce words depended on complex, gradually acquired physiological adaptations. Among these, for instance, is "the descended larynx" which, Donald explains, "leaves room for an elaborate supralaryngeal vocal apparatus that can create a greatly increased variety of sounds" (102). Also, among humans a distinctive curvature at the base of the skull affects the muscles of the pharynx as well as its high positioning and the development of a long tongue and soft palate that are "characteristic only of modern humans" (101). Developments such as these provided the physical foundation that made our unique, rapid symbolic speech possible, and there is a broad consensus that the crucial period was some 200,000 to 150,000 years ago – which, as Donald says, makes human speech as we know it today a surprisingly recent development.

As I mentioned earlier, it is interesting to consider why the australopithecines chose to live on the savanna, especially given that predation was an ever-present threat with which the plodding *Australopithicus* was not well equipped to deal. But, as Donald (citing Lovejoy) explains, there were gains: "The presence of bipedal locomotion in australopithecines signaled the emergence of a characteristically human family structure, with an increase in birth rate and group size, social stability, and social cooperation in raising young and obtaining food" (105).

That is, the australopithecines gambled that their vulnerability would be offset by the social advantages afforded by living closely together. Their ability to communicate was probably confined to rudimentary vocalizations and gestures, but the fact that they became bipedal resulted in the further evolution of their feet, hands, respiratory tracts, necks, spines, and pelvises. In turn, these developments laid the groundwork for the distinctive organization of the pharynx, tongue, and palate that eventually enabled speech as we now know it. Also, the fact that australopithecines lived in small groups and co-operated in raising offspring indicates that they placed a higher value on parental care than was the case among the great apes. The result is, as Bellah says, that humans have evolved as an altricial species to a degree unmatched by any other animals. That is, our young are helpless at birth (in contrast to precocial species, whose young are more developed at birth and more quickly able to look after themselves).[23] Citing Sarah Hrdy, Bellah writes that, over time, extended parental care led to increased intelligence, sociability, and empathy – especially the "advanced empathy" described by de Waal, whereby children come to understand that others have the "same kind of feelings" as they themselves do, and should be treated accordingly (68–69).

In her book *The Philosophical Baby*, Alison Gopnik[24] makes this same general point about extended parental care. The nurturing of babies dissolves "the boundaries between self and others", and we develop empathy through our early "face-to-face interactions" (208). Gopnik shows that babies are surprisingly empathetic, pretty much from the moment they are born. Without yet being capable of self-recognition, they imitate facial expressions and are "born knowing that particular facial expressions reflect particular kinesthetic feelings". It seems that "an innate empathetic link between babies and other people" (205) is already hardwired and geared to calling up in adults a reciprocal response. As Gopnik goes on to say, "my immediate, deep, selfless, uncalculating care for this particular baby, and the baby's love and care for me, are rooted in evolutionary imperatives" (208). And so the hazardous adventure of the australopithecines some 4 million years ago took a chance that a new model of parental care was the way of the future, and despite some bad odds, they were right about that. Consequently, we might find good evidence already 4 million years ago of our extraordinary investment in empathy as a survival strategy. This is one reason why, as Levinas, Bellah, and Gopnik confirm, the countenance of the other already makes a moral demand and exerts a moral force even before reflection and before speech.

The australopithecine way of life seems not to have differed greatly from that of *Homo habilis*, except that the habilines made tools, and for that reason are designated *Homo*. As I have mentioned, the picture is a great deal clearer with *Homo erectus*, who came on the scene some 1.5 million years ago. *Erectus* developed much more sophisticated tools (axes, choppers, cleavers, scrapers) than the habilines, while also carrying forward the stable social patterns developed by the australopithecines. But unlike the australopithecines, *Homo erectus* migrated across the globe, from Africa to Europe and Asia, and was, as Donald says, "a completely different creature, in terms of adaptability and cognitive resources from any that preceded". Citing Lieberman, Donald concludes that the physiology of *erectus* was not yet well enough developed to produce the sounds necessary for complex speech. This point is confirmed by the fact that the tool kit developed by *erectus* stayed remarkably stable for almost 2 million years. By contrast, the astonishingly rapid technological advances achieved by *Homo sapiens* were enabled especially by the acquisition of complex spoken language. And yet, as Donald argues, there must have been an intermediate stage before the emergence of language, during which communication was sufficiently complex to explain the achievements of *erectus* culture. Donald refers to this level of communication as "mimetic", by which he means "the ability to produce conscious, self-initiated, representational acts that are intentional but not linguistic" (168). Examples are "tones of voice, facial expressions, eye movements, manual signs and gestures, postural attitudes, patterned whole-body movements of various sorts" (169). As a moment's reflection confirms, the mimetic dimension of language remains very much with us today. It is central to how trades are learned and apprenticeships served, and, as Donald goes on to say, it is "at the very center of the arts" (169) – as we see, for instance, in dance, music, painting, theatre, cinema, and opera. Many modern art forms present a rich interplay between mimetic and narrative modes of expression, and the deeply embodied, direct power of mimetic representation remains a fundamental aspect of how we communicate in daily life. As Bellah says, our "total bodily relation to reality is never lost" (19), and "if conceptual representation is not reintegrated with the other forms of representation, then serious distortion may occur" (39).

Across some 2 million or so years of evolution involving an as yet uncharted variety of species living in widely dispersed locations across the globe, it is impossible to be clear about the exact processes by which spoken language meshed with already well-advanced mimetic forms of communication and other advanced cognitive skills to produce the complexities that characterize our communications today. But it is probable that in the great variety of hunter-gatherer groups preceding the Agricultural Revolution some 10,000 years ago, there were hundreds of languages, innumerable local divinities, and a vast abundance of stories about the origins and place of people in the world. Something of the poetry and symbolic power of the oral traditions within which mythic thinking was transmitted remains in the ancient epics that emerged from those traditions with the advent of writing, such as the *Iliad* and the *Odyssey*, the oldest strata of the Bible, and the Indian *Mahabharata*. But as we see also in these texts, myth is taken up into extended narratives, becoming part of a longer story that deals with the formation of cultural identity over time. As Bellah writes, "human beings are narrative creatures", and narrativity "is at the heart of our identity" (34). Just so, in oral tradition the special service rendered by the bards and hierophants who recited from memory was to be a storage system for a narrative about the society at large, so that social order and cultural identity could be better understood and preserved. But the memory banks of the dedicated retainers of the old myths and stories became less indispensable with the advent of writing and the making of permanent records. As I mentioned in the Introduction, one enduring fascination of Plato's *Dialogues* is that they demonstrate an uneasy, sometimes fraught interplay between orality (face-to-face exchange) and written discourse (a record of solitary philosophical reflection). And yet, throughout, there is a special excitement in the new process of ideas finding stability through writing, as conceptual argument takes us beyond myth and narrative towards a realm of ideal forms which merge then also, for Plato, with the idea of a Supreme Good.

In general, the pioneering thinkers of the Axial Age, such as Plato, taught that adherence to a transcendent world of universals should take priority over the traditional bonds of family, cult, and primordial kinship systems – that is, over the ages-old consolidations that mythic culture had done much to bring about by way of powerful metaphors and narratives stressing our embeddedness and participation in the enduring rhythms of nature. The Axial Age is also sometimes described as having discovered and developed second-order thinking – that is, thinking about the process of thinking itself, which in turn engenders rules and principles that stay stable in an otherwise shifting and illusory world. As Elkana[25] points out, the study of geometry in ancient Greece is a good example of Axial Age innovation, and in that light it is perhaps not surprising that a sign outside Plato's Academy (purportedly) declared, "Let no one ignorant of geometry enter here".

The characteristic two-tiered model of the universe pioneered by the Axial Age thinkers remains very much present in the major world religions today, but as our present state of knowledge allows us also to see, a plurality of teachings, each claiming to have exclusive access to a single transcendent truth, can hardly coexist comfortably. One solution made broadly available by secularism is to dismantle the two-tiered model itself on the grounds that the world immediately present in all its material variety and impenetrability is quite enough, thank you. Not surprisingly, a good deal of modern art is strongly drawn to ancient, pre-Axial cultures and religions. For secular modernism, that is, the direct connection between the old religions and the rhythms of nature dispenses with oppressive, abstract doctrines based on aspirations to an otherworldly transcendence. The modern interest in primitive religions is therefore not so much regressive as a self-conscious, mainly secular attempt to get rid of the two-tiered structures introduced during the Axial Age. Because this self-consciousness is a product of modern times, there is no question of the actual sensibilities of our hunter-gatherer forebears somehow being recovered. Rather, the old myths are evoked to remind us of values with which we have lost contact under the influence of the Axial Age abstractions, and in turn, these values can be a corrective to a society that has become excessively instrumental in its attitudes to nature and other people.

Modern secular skepticism notwithstanding, however, the shaping force of the Axial Age remains profound, and as Eisenstadt convincingly argues, it has had "far-reaching implications for the formation of the human personality".[26] This is so because people have so often sought to conform their innermost selves, as well as their behavior, to transcendent standards against which their lives would by and by be judged. The conflict between ideal standards and universal aspirations on the one hand and passionate bonds and primordial loyalties on the other can be intense, and even, as the Greeks realized, tragic. And so Antigone is torn by the conflict between what she is bound to do by the ties of kinship and what the law prescribes. A further extensive body of European literature grows out of analogous, tragic tensions (*Tristan and Iseult, Romeo and Juliet, Madame Bovary, The End of the Affair*), as well as from tensions that stop short of or go beyond tragedy, as in Augustine's *Confessions*, Dante's *Divine Comedy*, and Milton's *Paradise Lost*. In these examples as well as countless others, the contest and interplay between different values and desires are held in a dynamic equilibrium that constitutes the power of the work of art to engage us. Just so, the genius of Plato, Jesus, and the Buddha is not adequately described by an account of their ideas and doctrines. The real life of the dialogues, the gospels, and the sutras lies in the vivid, dialogical engagement between a teacher and a variety of interlocutors whose partial understandings, prejudices, feelings, insights, and individual circumstances are the context within which the teachings can engage the deeper affective and tacit layers of people's understanding so that new knowledge can become a matter of personal conviction rather than just a set of doctrines. This does not mean that doctrines and principles are unimportant. Rather, the analytical thinking that developed since the Axial Age remains indispensable today, even though we ought not to lose sight of the fact that its emergence is part of a larger, more complex story.

Openings: personal, political, religious

So far, I have suggested that dialogue is initiated as a response to the other whose appearance makes a primordial demand, reaching into the pre-articulate depths of our sentient and intentional selves and calling for us to set aside self-interest in order to attend to and respond to the other. Dialogue, which begins with this response, relies then for its continuance on the evolved complexity of the communication skills that I have outlined and through which we are most fully present to the other who is like us even though also inalienably different. And yet the oldest, deepest drive of all, the drive for self-preservation, pulls us all too compellingly away from a disposition to self-abnegating hospitality, as the impulses to self-assertion and power take over as the means by which we seek to acquire dominance and, therefore, invulnerability. This is the "natural man" – the "old man" of Pauline theology – and the conflict between egocentrism and a self-abdicating care for the other recurs at every phase of human history and in every individual human life. Levinas describes it as an opposition between Totality and Infinity.[27] On the one hand, a totalizing panoptic vision aims to contain and control; on the other hand, we aspire to an infinitely open-ended, multicentered, creative exchange. Bakhtin makes an analogous distinction in describing the difference between monological and dialogical discourses.[28] Monologue is self-contained and brooks no interruption; by contrast, dialogue is open-ended and thrives on an interplay among different points of view.

Today, it is not difficult to recognize in a great deal of public discourse on which side of this set of alternatives the main emphasis falls, as a pandemonium of monologues, a congeries of totalizing individual opinions pitting each against all, communicate for the most part a failure to communicate. Driven by an exaggerated competitiveness and an insatiable consumerism, all this could hardly be further removed from the spirit of dialogue that assumes, as Alain Badiou says (in concert here with Levinas and Bakhtin), that the other is not just external but is part of one's own self-constitution.[29] The good of others is therefore also one's own good. By contrast, a politics designed to support the prevailing creed of each against all yields merely a parodic inversion of community; a juxtaposition, that is, of monads in perpetual, negative interdependence.

Insofar as we might feel inclined to turn our attention once more to the overarching enigma – the cosmic mystery beyond the personal and the political – again the cold yet bracing comfort is that there is no final word, and any religious faith worth taking seriously coexists with a continued pondering of the doubts that reason presents to belief, as Thomas Aquinas pointed out long ago.[30] In turn, dialogue comes into its own as a response along these several fronts to this same, perennial, open-ended uncertainty.

Recapitulation and the uses of literature

Dialogue, then, engages the full range of the communication skills acquired through the course of our cultural evolution. In every face-to-face encounter the body already conveys complex information, and an extensive range of shared, expressive gestures is virtually universal among humans.[31] The vocalized sounds that Darwin called "primordial song" remain today an efficient means of expressing basic emotions – the music of the voice, that is, as distinct from its phonetic repertoire. The ability to invent myths and narratives that subsequently developed with spoken language is also indispensable today, not least because in order to make sense of events we need to tell stories about them. The Axial Age advances in conceptual thought that subjected mythic and narrative thinking to critical scrutiny placed a high value on analytical reason and led by and by to the development of modern science and the emergence of secularism. Yet Axial Age clashes between rational argument and traditional myths and narratives continue to persist, and occur today in virtually every country in the world. And so the conceptual does not shake itself entirely loose from those aspects of tradition that shape what we take to be our identity, whether individual or cultural, just as traditional myths and narratives are inseparable from the prelinguistic ties and sympathies that bind us to one another at a pre-articulate level. These layered strategies for communication remain interdependent though also sometimes at odds with one another, but we cannot dispense with any of them without compromising some significant aspect of who and what we are as persons. And so I have suggested that dialogue enables us to understand the implicit relationship between the personal and the political, as well as the usefulness and limits of religious language. Because dialogue recalls us to this complex state of affairs, it is much more than merely an exchange of ideas and opinions, even though ideas and opinions remain part of it.

In his book about dialogue, David Bohm[32] also emphasizes that the process he wants to describe is more than an exchange of, or a contest between, opinions. He suggests that because ideas and concepts are general, we can stand back during a dialogical exchange and follow the thinking process more or less objectively as it unfolds, without forcing our individual point of view, despite whatever feelings might prompt us to do so. And yet, Bohm does not claim that dialogue is impersonal, and he draws on Michael Polanyi to confirm that, however abstract, thinking is never entirely disconnected from the embodied complexities of the thinker. As Hans-Georg Gadamer points out, language contains all kinds of evaluations and prejudgements ("prejudices", that is) that shape our address to the world and that we cannot simply step outside. Consequently, in standing back to observe and follow the process of thinking, we are likely to discover prejudices that we had not realized were part of our personal narrative. Gadamer describes the exchange of ideas, narratives, and feelings as a "fusion of horizons"[33] that can go on opening up, as with dialogue itself, without final closure. In order to clarify the point, he appeals to our experience of art, which he holds to be fundamentally dialogical. As I explained in Chapter 1, in a book such as this, confined as it is to the written word, literature is the form of art that best exemplifies the "fusion of horizons" that Gadamer describes as the modus operandi of dialogue itself. Here it might then be pertinent briefly to clarify what I take to be the usefulness of literature and criticism in a study such as this.

Since the late 19th century, the idea that literature offers instruction not by prescription but by giving us insight into the quality of our lives has become commonplace. This broadly Arnoldian view was the cornerstone of a revival of English studies in England in the early 20th century, as is clear in the landmark 1921 UK Board of Education report *The Teaching of English in England*,[34] usually referred to as the Newbolt Report (after Henry Newbolt, who chaired the committee). The report recommends an education rooted in the national literature, and seeks to establish education more deeply in the "common life" of the national culture. Universities are to become "ambassadors of poetry", teachers are described as missionaries, and literature is declared "one of the chief temples of the human spirit, in which all should worship". The Arnoldian idea that literature would replace religion in a modern secular culture is entirely clear here, and it was a short step then to F.R. Leavis (1895–1978), who saw literature as promoting humane values in an overly industralized and commercialized society. In short, the Newbolt Report helped to shape Leavis's conviction that an education in English literature by way of a "great tradition"[35] of key works is a life-enhancing antidote to a soulless culture. As Terry Eagleton says, students of English today (especially in the United Kingdom) remain Leavisites "whether they know it or not, irremediably altered by that historic intervention",[36] and through the New Criticism the same broad preoccupations pervaded the classrooms of transatlantic universities as well. Subsequently, from roughly the last third of the 20th century, the fact that literary studies turned sharply toward theory is hardly surprising, given the flimsy underpinnings of the idea that literature makes us, somehow, better persons. Questions and responses flooded in, as they still do, from a wide range of disciplines – semiotics, psychoanalysis, Marxism, feminism, structuralism, phenomenology, and others. But in the midst of this many-sided debate, one point about Leavis's agenda that is often passed over remains pertinent to what I want to say about dialogue.

For Leavis, that is, discerning and thoughtful reading can clarify what is valuable about literature by showing how its strategies operate, both structurally (structure conveys meaning) and by way of the various narrative, symbolic, and prosodic effects to which literary critics attend. Critical reflection therefore enables us better to understand the felt complexities of our response to a text as an experience that we can fruitfully assess by patient recollection and through using language adequate to the task as we engage with the text dialogically, as Gadamer explains. In short, what I have said about the Axial Age in relation to myth and narrative is what I am now saying also about criticism and literature. Just as there is a continuing, dialogical exchange between the second-order, conceptual thinking of the Axial Age and the mythic, narrative aspects of the cultures it addresses, so there is a dialogue between the conceptual apparatus of criticism and the mythic, narrative aspects of the texts upon which criticism reflects. Literature is often mythic; it can dramatize or otherwise represent the mimetic; it depends heavily on narrative; and by way of metaphor, symbol, and the music of language, it reaches into the recesses of the body to awaken responses that lie deeper than words. But literature also explores ideas, and thereby opens up within itself a dialogue between the conceptual and the figurative, of which discerning readers take account as they engage with the entire process of recapitulation that is indispensable to the authentic experience and practice of dialogue. In attempting to understand better these layers of engagement and response, critical reflection can therefore make conscious some aspects of how we are affected by what we read – a process that reason cannot fully explain, but about which it can provide some insight and understanding that in turn can be shared and discussed. Reading well in this fashion is a skill that requires patience and discernment, as well as a respect for evidence, and the same is true, analogously, for dialogue. A society that depends on a high degree of literacy in order to function would do well to ensure that these skills continue to be valued and developed.

I began this chapter by noting that the scientists who in 2018 moved the Doomsday Clock forward are rightfully worried about the dangers of failing to communicate well, and about an erosion of discourse in the public sphere. In 1946, George Orwell worried about the same thing. In response, he wrote that language "becomes ugly and inaccurate because our thoughts are foolish, but the slovenliness of language makes it easier for us to have foolish thoughts. The point is that the process is reversible. Modern English, especially written English, is full of bad habits which spread by imitation and which can be avoided if one is willing to take the necessary trouble. If one gets rid of these habits one can think more clearly, and to think clearly is a necessary first step towards political regeneration: so that the fight against bad English is not frivolous and is not the exclusive concern of professional writers".[37] Orwell thought that the bad habits were reversible. Among other things, he did not foresee the high-speed contagion and diversity of today's digital communications and the effects these are having on reading practices and on the reading brain, the immense benefits of the new technologies notwithstanding. Would he be so confident now? Maybe less so, and yet, I'm guessing, not entirely not.

Notes

1 Doomsday Clock, *Bulletin of the Atomic Scientists*, 2018 statement, ed. John Mecklin. www.the bulletin.org.
2 Martin Buber, "Distance and Relation", in *The Knowledge of Man. Selected Essays*, trans. Ronald Gregor Smith, ed. Maurice Friedman (New York: Harper and Row, 1965), p. 69.
3 Maryanne Wolf, "Skim Reading Is the New Normal. The Effect on Society is Profound", *The Guardian*, August 25, 2018; *Reader, Come Home. The Reading Brain in a Digital World* (New York: Harper Collins, 2018), pp. 47, 50. Wolf cites Sherry Turkle as attributing the loss of empathy largely to the inability of young people "to navigate the online world without losing track of their real-time, face-to-face relationships" (50). For an account of the differences between navigating printed and on-screen texts, see Ferris Jabr, "The Reading Brain in the Digital Age: The Science of Paper versus Screens", Scientific American, April 11, 2013.
4 Rachel Bronson, president and CEO of the Bulletin of the Atomic Scientists, commenting on the 2018 statement. For a thoughtful assessment of the far-reaching implications of this problem, see Tom Nichols, *The Death of Expertise: The Campaign against Established Knowledge and Why it Matters* (Oxford: Oxford University Press, 2017).
5 Charles Taylor, *A Secular Age* (Harvard: Harvard University Press, 2007), p. 21.
6 See Patrick Grant, *Literature of Mysticism in Western Tradition* (London: Macmillan, 1983), pp. 8–10, 143.
7 David Hume, *Dialogues Concerning Natural Religion* (1779), p. 63.
8 A compelling account of this convergence is provided by Richard Dawkins, *The Greatest Show on Earth. The Evidence for Evolution* (London: Bantam, 2009).
9 See, for example, *The City of God*, Book XI, chapter 7.

10 The Creation Museum in Petersburg, Kentucky, is a good example, as a visit to its website quickly shows. A guide to creation museums is available online at http://visitcreation.org.

11 Northrop Frye, *The Great Code. The Bible and Literature* (Toronto: Academic Press, 1982), pp. 37 ff.

12 Robert Alter, *The Art of Biblical Narrative* (New York: Basic Books, 1981), pp. 141 ff.

13 Paul Feyerabend, *Against Method* (London: New Left Books, 1975), puts the case for science proceeding in a highly eclectic manner. See also Patrick Grant, *Literature and the Discovery of Method in the English Renaissance* (London: Macmillan, 1985), pp. 6ff.

14 Robert N. Bellah, *Religion in Human Evolution. From the Paleolithic to the Axial Age* (Harvard: Harvard University Press, 2011), p. 600.

15 The following summary draws especially on Jerry A. Coyne, *Why Evolution Is True* (New York: Viking, 2009); Dawkins, *The Greatest Show on Earth. The Evidence for Evolution;* Donald R. Prothero, *Evolution: What the Fossils Say and Why It Matters* (New York: Columbia University Press, 2017); *Evolution: The Whole Story*, ed. Steve Parker, foreword, Alice Walker (London: Thames and Hudson, 2015). The website of The Smithsonian Institution's Human Origins Program is especially helpful.

16 See Eric Gans, *The Origin of Language: A Formal Theory of Representation* (Berkeley: University of California Press, 1981); René Girard, *Violence and the Sacred*, trans. Patrick Gregory (Baltimore: Johns Hopkins University Press, 1977). Gans adopts and develops Girard's thinking about "mimetic desire" and violence.

17 Karl Jaspers, *The Origin and Goal of History*, trans. Michael Bullock (London: Routledge and Kegan Paul, 1953). The following account draws also on *The Origins and Diversity of Axial Age Civilizations,* ed. S. N. Eisenstadt (Albany: State University of New York Press, 1986), and *The Axial Age and Its Consequences*, ed. Robert N. Bellah and Hans Joas (Cambridge, Massachusetts: Harvard University Press, 2012).

18 See *Totality and Infinity. An Essay on Exteriority*, trans. Alphonso Lingis (Pittsburg: Duquesne University Press, 1969), pp. 79 ff. These basic ideas are woven throughout Levinas' writings. For example, see *Otherwise than Being or Beyond Essence*, trans. Alphonso Lingis (Dordrecht and Boston: Kluwer Academic Publishers, 1978), and *Humanism of the Other*, trans. Nidra Poller (Urbana and Chicago: University of Illinois Press, 2006, first published, 1972).

19 Plato, *Letter* VII, 341 c-e, 344 b-d.

20 *Republic*, 350 d; 358 c-d.

21 The central work is *Personal Knowledge. Towards a Post-Critical Philosophy* (New York: Harper and Row, 1964. First published, 1958).

22 Merlin Donald, *Origins of the Modern Mind. Three Stages in the Evolution of Culture and Cognition* (Cambridge, Mass.: Harvard University Press, 1991); Bellah, *Religion in Human Evolution. From the Paleolithic to the Axial Age.* Page numbers are cited in the text.

23 As Robert N. Bellah points out. *See Religion in Human Evolution*, p. 68.

24 Alison Gopnik, *The Philosophical Baby. What Children's Minds Tell Us About Truth, Love, and the Meaning of Life* (New York: Ferrar, Straus and Giroux, 2009). Page numbers are cited in the text.

25 Yehuda Elkana "The Emergence of Second-Order Thinking in Classical Greece", in *The Origins and Diversity of Axial Age Civilizations*, ed. S. N. Eisenstadt, pp. 58 ff.
26 S. N. Eisenstadt, "The Axial Age Breakthroughs – Their Characteristics and Origins", in *The Origins and Diversity of Axial Age Civilizations*, p. 5.
27 See *Totality and Infinity*.
28 Mikhail Bakhtin, *Problems of Dostoevsky's Poetics*, ed. and trans. Caryl Emerson (Minneapolis: University of Minnesota Press, 1984). Michael Holquist, *Dialogism: Bakhtin and His World* (London: Routledge, 1990), provides a thoughtful and clear account of Bakhtin's ideas.
29 Alain Badiou, *I Know There Are So Many of You*, trans. Susan Spitzer (Cambridge: Polity Press, 2019), pp. 33–34.
30 See *Summa Theologiae*, ST 2a 2ae, 2, 1, and 2a 2ae 1, 2.
31 See Donald, *Origins of the Modern Mind*, 220 ff.
32 David Bohm, *On Dialogue* (London: Routledge, 2013), pp. 21, 51, 52.
33 Hans-Georg Gadamer, *Truth and Method*, translation revised by Joel Weinsheimer and Donald G. Marshall (London: Bloomsbury Academic, 2013; first published, 1975), pp. 282–94, 317, 382.
34 *The Teaching of English in England* (London: HM Stationery Office, 1921), p. 289.
35 See *The Great Tradition* (London: Chatto and Windus, 1960; first published, 1948).
36 Terry Eagleton, *Literary Theory. An Introduction* (Oxford: Basil Blackwell, 1983), p. 31.
37 George Orwell, "Politics and the English Language", *Selected Essays* (Harmondsworth: Penguin, 1957; first published, 1946), p. 143.

3 Being not unrecognized

The same and the different

Dialogue begins, then, with the response of a listener who sets aside self-interest in order to participate in a further, shared exchange. A refusal of dialogue is therefore marked first by a refusal to listen, and then also by a refusal to think along with others in a spirit of willing participation. Shakespeare's Cleopatra doesn't exactly refuse to listen to the messenger who brings bad news, but in verbally abusing him and then having him physically mistreated she could hardly be described as setting aside self-interest in order to further the exchange. And yet, how familiar the "Cleopatra response" is today in all manner of public exchanges. How normal it has become to listen to people talking insistently over each other, set on the promotion of already-established convictions that are rendered then all the more obdurate by denouncing whatever messengers are the bearers of different or otherwise unpleasing news. And when the messengers on all sides are equally intent on playing Cleopatra, the result is a collision of monologues, a clash of egos, a hubbub in which nothing is learned.

By contrast, the participants in dialogue take a chance in attending unselfishly to their interlocutors, and what is learned then emerges unpredictably. But participation does not mean uncritical immersion, and requires an acknowledgment also of the inalienable difference of the other. As Thomas Browne reminded us long ago, "no man truely knowes another",[1] but it is the case nonetheless that someone wholly different – a wholly isolated individual – would not long be viable, and our continuance as a species has depended on co-operation based on a shared sameness.[2] That is, as members of a species we are interdependent, and the needs of our species-being are not met without co-operation. Since the development of civilization in the centuries following the Agricultural Revolution, however, the ways in which human societies are organized hardly reflect our fundamental equality, and the idea of people "working together" has often meant that an indentured, or inferior, or enslaved class labors to serve the interests of a powerful elite. Is there a way, then, for people to live and work interdependently without subjection and in a manner that serves the common good, while also acknowledging individual difference?

Dialogue in itself is not the answer, because dialogue does not effect political change and a thoroughly dialogical politics is hardly feasible, given the adversarial nature of politics as we know it. Yet dialogue offers a manner of engaging with others by way of thoughtful participation on many fronts in our personal and civic lives. In a participatory democracy, some broadly shared understanding of the dialogical process – promoted by education and by everyday practice – would provide a context of informed ideas, critically assessed and freely produced, and within which political decisions could then best be made. It follows that a fully participatory democracy would also place the highest value on dialogue. By contrast, as I proposed in Chapter 1, today's widely extolled individualism promotes itself as the guarantor of free self-determination and equality of opportunity, whereas in fact the individual has become more than ever an isolated unit, afforded the illusory freedom of "working together" within an economic system that privileges the few and extols self-interest as the principal criterion of success. This kind of negative interdependency is nothing better than a parody of the freedom that it undertakes to promote, as it replaces dialogue with a mere clash of isolated contending opinions, while political power remains concentrated in the hands of the few who also have economic power.

Still, it is worth recalling that a great variety of dissenting initiatives in a broad range of political and social contexts continue to promote alternative possibilities,[3] though it is discouraging also to realize how daunting the impediments to fundamental change actually are. It is simply hard to see how today's corporate capitalism, with its adjuncts – militarism, the fetishizing of greed, and the grotesque accumulation of wealth by a tiny percentage of the population – can be reformed from within. Consequently, the idea of dialogue that I am presenting here is sadly insufficient against the juggernaut – as if a verbal gesture might dissuade Goliath. Nonetheless, as Plato insisted from the start, the values inherent in dialogue ought to go on being instilled, especially by education, if only because they are not irrelevant to what the republic might and should become, however impervious the oligarchs and tyrants still appear to be.

Imagining the immanence of others

So far, I have suggested that participation in dialogue depends on an acknowledgement that the other is like us even though also irreducibly different. On the one hand, an overemphasis on difference produces an exaggerated individualism – the negative interdependency that pits each against all and reduces dialogue to a series of competing monologues. On the other hand, an overemphasis on sameness results in a faceless collectivity. There is no formula for balancing these alternatives, which is why dialogue remains an art rather than a set of prescriptions. Yet it is also the case that the exaggerated value placed on individualism in the name of free enterprise makes it especially easy today to ignore the fact that the other is not merely an object set over against us, and to acknowledge the other as already to some degree constitutive of our own identity. As Alain Badiou writes, "Otherness is immanent in all identity, which means that I am only myself insofar as I am the Other of that Other for whom I am myself. There's no getting around this, and it is the real foundation of freedom".[4] As we shall see, Mikhail Bakhtin insists also that the other is at the heart of the subject I take myself to be, and consequently only through dialogue it is possible for people to think together in a manner that prevails over individual self-interest. Still, the fact remains that the other is also an individual who is not fully accessible, and the process of mutual exchange and discovery is therefore never concluded, never finalized.

These points about participation and the displacement of self-interest in the process of creative discovery are standard tropes also in discussions about imagination, a topic which it is now helpful to consider briefly as a means of clarifying how the immanence of the other in our own identity pertains to an understanding of dialogue.

Especially since Immanuel Kant, it has become commonplace to acknowledge that the human mind does not look upon the world neutrally. Rather, as Kant proposes, the mind configurates, so that when we perceive objects we partly construct them. Kant does not say that our thinking and perceiving constitute the world (that would be solipsism), just as he does not say that our minds are a neutral recording apparatus. We know actual things (the noumena) by way of our specifically human means of perceiving and understanding, but we do not know things as they are in themselves (the phenomena). Kant refers to the synthesizing processes at work in perception as "productive imagination", in contrast to the "reproductive imagination" that occurs when we deliberately conjure up an image in our minds.[5] This distinction was highly influential on Samuel Taylor Coleridge

(1772–1834), the main philosopher of the imagination in Romantic England. Based on Kant, Coleridge[6] proposes a distinction between the "primary" and "secondary" functions of imagination. That is, the synthesizing activity by which our perceptions organize the world is itself a kind of thinking, though we are usually unaware of it as such, and this is "primary imagination". When we proceed deliberately to invent images we deploy "secondary imagination", which, in poetry for instance, creates new meanings through metaphor, imagery, and so on, allowing us to experience and understand our interconnectedness with the world in new ways. Coleridge also distinguishes between imagination and fancy, which merely juxtaposes similarities without tapping into nature's living power and vitality. By contrast, true imagination is "a repetition in the finite mind of the eternal act of creation in the infinite I AM".[7] Here Coleridge's thinking opens directly onto religion, as he claims that through imagination the mind discovers its affinity not only with the creative energies of nature but also with God, the first creator.

The line of transmission from Kant and the Romantics to the phenomenologists, Heidegger, post-structuralism, and deconstruction preserves the idea of the mind's shaping and configurative activity, while emphasizing also that human subjectivity is itself shaped or constructed – for instance, through language and culture. One result of this broad course of development is that in the modernist phase, the idea of God as the transcendent source in whose image we are made is much less readily affirmed by theories about the creative imagination than was the case for Coleridge. God, rather, seems also to be a construction, an imagined ideal of wholeness, unity, salvation. And so Jacques Lacan asks, "Is the *one* anterior to discontinuity?" To which he replies: "I do not think so, and everything I have taught in recent years has tended to exclude this need for a closed *one*".[8] For Lacan, that is, Coleridge's "finite mind" through which the creative act takes place is misrecognized as having an affinity with "the infinite I AM", the God who is another desired object to which we aspire as we go on endlessly trying to reclaim for ourselves our earliest imagined experiences of union and identity. For Lacan, Romantic-inspired notions about the blissful unitary experience of infants are misguided, and he stresses instead that infants are uncoordinated, helpless, and often terrified. Also, infants spend a lot of time gazing and hearing, and they take comfort from the fact that, by looking at other people, they imagine the body as a totality with which they seek to identify in order to find solace and reassurance. From earliest childhood, humans are therefore aware of a unified, external form of another body, even while experiencing themselves as internally fragmented and confused.

At approximately six months of age, Lacan says, an infant comes to see others as it would see itself in a mirror, as a unified image. At this "mirror stage" the mother is especially important, because the child's earliest bonding with her is a main bulwark against chaos and anxiety. Later in life, further images of a desirable, protective wholeness are encountered in others whom we imagine also as being whole or unified. Even as adults, our idealizing misrecognitions continue to be fueled by imagination and by desires that bring us all the way back to infancy, when a longed-for union with the mother was a necessary strategy for managing our helplessness and vulnerability.

According to Lacan, as a child develops, separation from the mother occurs in the interests of the child's social development. The main agent of this traumatic separation from the mother is language, through which a speaker enters the "symbolic" order of culture. In turn, language entails a consciousness of standing apart, and Lacan draws on Saussure's theory that meaning emerges from within language by way of differences among signifiers rather than through an identity between words and their referents. For Lacan, words therefore never fill the gap between our aspirations to wholeness or fullness of meaning and what we are actually able to say. In the gap between the body and language, which reconfigures the gap between the imaginary and the symbolic, desire then springs up as the source of an unresolvable dissatisfaction and longing. The fact that desire never comes to rest in the search for meaning helps to explain why also, in dialogue, there is – and can be – no final word.

These remarks about imagination can help to clarify my opening suggestion in this chapter that dialogue avoids the extremes of individualism and collective anonymity on the grounds that the other is like us and also irreducibly different. Through the agency of imagination – which, according to Coleridge, is our ability to create meanings that reveal our interconnectedness with the world and with one another in new ways – we can better acknowledge the immanence of the other in what we take to be our own identity, and this is so because imagination is especially ordered to grasp how things can be single yet twofold (consider metaphor, for example). Also, through imagination we displace our point of view in order to see things from a different perspective, and as we have seen, dialogue likewise is impossible without some willingness to set self-centeredness in abeyance in order to see things from the point of view of the other. Imagination is a main means enabling us to do so, and in this light we can better understand how we have some limited capacity for self-fashioning, as, paradoxically, we become ourselves only through our relationships, which cannot be entirely separated from imagination. As Lacan adds, imagination also is fueled by desire that is perpetually unsatisfied in its search, through a series of misrecognitions and disappointments for an unattainable wholeness or union. Consequently, the misrecognitions and deceptions of imagination in turn influence our relationships. To develop these points about the process of our limited, dialogically based self-fashioning, I want to draw first on Hans-Georg Gadamer and then on Mikhail Bakhtin.

Gadamer: prejudgement and disclosure

Hans-Georg Gadamer (1900–2002)[9] writes extensively about dialogue, and his early training in classical philology and philosophy within a broadly neo-Kantian academic environment enabled him to read Plato's dialogues as a process of discovery rather than as a set of arguments to be assessed independently of a broader, dramatic representation of the mind's search for truth. Gadamer was also a student of Martin Heidegger (1889–1976), by whom he was strongly influenced.

Heidegger's "phenomenological hermeneutics" looks especially to early Greek philosophy for examples of speech that has not fallen victim to a post-Cartesian technological culture which habitually assumes a strong cleavage between subject and object. By contrast with Gadamer, Heidegger favors the Greek thinkers who preceded Plato – the pre-Socratics – in whom he finds an authentic speech in which Being is present to language in a manner that is now all but lost to us. Heidegger's entire philosophical project can then be thought of as an attempt to recover an authentic language that discloses the presentness of the Being that constitutes us and in which we participate, but from which we are alienated. To do this, he resorts to a recalcitrant, indirect form of writing designed to break through the sedimented clichés of conventional usage and to reveal with a fresh sense of wonder some new aspect of the mystery of Being in which we are immersed. Here philosophy becomes a kind of poetry, producing an effect of felt strangeness as we recover something of the familiar world anew in its primordial richness. It is important to notice that Heidegger undertakes consciously to recover the quality of an earlier, mythic language that prevailed in Greek philosophy before the intervention of the Axial Age abstractions that he attributes especially to Plato. As I suggested in Chapter 2, the value of dialogue today can best be understood as undertaking a similar, conscious recapitulation of earlier, key phases in the evolution of language, and I will return to this point by and by.

For now, as we see, Gadamer thought of Plato differently from Heidegger, but he nonetheless remains deeply influenced by Heidegger's[10] ideas about the power of disclosure, revelation, and the "unconcealedness" of truth that is discovered by indirection and by breaking through the sedimented clichés and assumptions built into day-to-day speech. But whereas Heidegger finds these qualities especially in the pre-Socratics, Gadamer finds them in Plato's dialogues, which he sees as a mimetic representation of the mind (or several minds) engaged in the passionate pursuit of truth that declares itself in the end as revelation, a quality of vision. The key difference between Gadamer and Heidegger is, therefore, that through Plato Gadamer develops Heidegger's phenomenological hermeneutics in the direction of the dialogical. As Donatella Di Cesare says, "the secret core of Gadamer's philosophy" is that it is "*a philosophy of dialogue*", and this is so not least because, as Gadamer frequently asserts, "language is dialogue".[11]

One effect of Gadamer's special interest in dialogue is, as it were, to blow fresh air through Heidegger's claustrophobic world. Gadamer's writing is more accessible, more in the mode of conversation than Heidegger's deliberate, cramped intensities. Yet both men share the basic idea that the human being (*Dasein*, "there being", in Heidegger's language) is "thrown" into a world that always already prepossesses us so that we are never simply positioned neutrally over against it. Rather, as Heidegger says, we are already participants who are called to engage the world through concern (*Sorge*), which in turn is a source of angst in the face of which we are to live courageously and authentically. The fact that we are not positioned neutrally but are always already shaped by our circumstances means also that we must expect our engagements with others to reveal our limitations, and this is not always easy to do. Here it is crucial to take account of the fact that language itself is one of those shaping circumstances, and it is indeed difficult to take account of how our thinking is formed by it. As Merlin Donald reminds us, "a collective lexicon is our inheritance, as surely as any set of genes", and through this inheritance we gain access to "society's symbolically held collective knowledge".[12] Along similar lines, in his book about dialogue David Bohm[13] writes that linguistically communicable thought belongs to the whole culture and is not the sole possession of individual speakers. He goes on to say that insofar as we imagine and understand how this is so, we recover a sense of the participatory consciousness that in fact is the foundation of human communication, however much we think of ourselves as independent subjects who are the initiators of the opinions we declare as our own. Rather, Bohm argues, we dwell in a common language just as a common language dwells in us as an embodied skill within which, as Michael Polanyi says, we move "as in the garment of our own skin".[14] Yet the "tacit dimension" from which the primary forms of cognition emerge remains as elusive as the origins of language itself, and although these primary processes can be elucidated, they cannot be adequately described. Maurice Merleau-Ponty writes that "speech always comes into play against a background of speech",[15] as language comprises a common stock of elements that are relatively stable – the dictionary definitions of words, for example – and yet every individual utterance is different and (it could be argued) never exactly repeatable because of the unique complexity of the circumstances in which it occurs. Consequently, the "background of speech" to which Merleau-Ponty refers and the particular speech coming into play in individual utterances remain in a constant, never-finalized exchange in which participatory sameness and irreducible difference interact and remain interdependent.

Some of Gadamer's most interesting ideas arise from his investigations of the same interplay between speech as "background" and speech "arising". Among these is the significance he attaches to prejudice, understood as prejudgement.[16] Because we are thrown into a specific situation on entering the world, our perspective is limited, but our limitations are also the indispensable background from which new understandings emerge. Because this is so, the idea of prejudgement has, for Gadamer, both a negative and a positive sense. On the one hand, it constitutes a bias, or prejudice, that can prevent communication. On the other hand, it is a necessary condition for communication, because our prejudgements constitute a frame of reference that enables us to speak meaningfully. Dialogue then is not a matter of individual opinion, but emerges from a broad range of what we believe, think, and feel, whether we realize it or not, as Merleau-Ponty, Bohm, and Polanyi are also at pains to demonstrate. It follows that any fruitful participation in dialogue will require the setting in abeyance of the monological ego to allow what Gadamer calls a "fusion of horizons".[17] That is, we participate in a process of thinking that reaches back through all the dimensions of our ability to communicate, reaching into the body's reflexes and deepest intentions, which the ego can never take fully into account if only because the part cannot fully comprehend the whole of which it is a part. New knowledge and enhanced understanding emerge when, through a fusion of horizons, our personal kaleidoscope shifts so that, mediated by our interlocutor's different frame of reference, a new, self-authenticating constellation of ideas, insights, and understandings comes to light.

Just as dialogue remains endlessly open, so the fusion of horizons modifies and transforms unpredictably the views we bring to bear with each new encounter. For Gadamer, as for Heidegger, truth then is a disclosure, a showing forth of some new understanding about which the participants agree. And yet this disclosure occurs only when I come up against the limits of my view of the world – my horizon – through encountering the other who is different but who is willing also to interrogate the prejudgements that inform our separate though overlapping views of the world. Prejudices then emerge (perhaps, even, are discovered) and become the opportunity for unexpected transformations and new integrations. In this context, Gadamer writes appreciatively about friendship,[18] which (among other things) is what Plato means by the spirit of dialogue, the underpinning of mutual goodwill that accepts difference in order to respond generously to the summons of the other, as Levinas says, so that the exchange can continue without prejudice pre-empting openness. And yet, the fact remains, as always, that there is no final word, no perfect merging of horizons, but rather the continuing life of the dialogue itself. As Jean Grondin writes, citing Gadamer's "The Limits of Language", we want "to know the word which can reach the other" but we always know at the same time that we have "not completely found it", and this "*unsatisfying* search for the *mot juste* constitutes life proper, and the essence of language".[19] It is easy to recognize here the common experience of how words fall short of making the human contact we desire, and how often we feel the pressure of knowing more than we can say. And yet there are also moments of recognition, disclosure, understanding, "gleams and fractions"[20] that occur through and across the enduring gaps and imperfections, and of which dialogue is, pre-eminently, the vehicle.

How dialogue imitates art

In light of these remarks, it is no surprise that Gadamer[21] looks to art as a paradigm of how truth occurs, and this is so at least partly because in art, as in dialogue, the process of response and interpretation requires our co-operative engagement, while remaining open-ended. Also, Gadamer's dialogical view of art places him in firm opposition to the reduction of art to the aesthetics of taste (on the Kantian model), and he insists instead on reinserting art into a rougher, many-sided discourse where moral and intellectual concerns fuse within our experience of the beautiful. Thus, we might well be moved by the wonderful, often piercing language of *King Lear,* but the play teaches us as well about ingratitude, cruelty, and love in the actual world. The opening section of Gadamer's *Truth and Method* is entitled "The Question of Truth as It Emerges in the Experience of Art", and what he sets out there remains fundamental to the rest of the book.

For Gadamer, that is, art does not offer the same face-to-face dialogical encounter as does meeting another person, but it nonetheless has its own subjectivity in which we are invited to participate. And so a fusion of horizons occurs in our engagement with a work of art, which, through its particular medium, discloses some aspect of the familiar world, showing us what we thought we knew already but now in a different light and as an unanticipated dimension of being that we recognize and affirm as true and through which our personal horizon is expanded or transfigured.

And yet, more clearly than is the case with the other whom we meet face-to-face, art addresses us from within the strict limits imposed by its material medium. Here a consideration arises on which Gadamer does not directly dwell, namely that great art contrives also to thematize its own limitations, its own necessary imperfection, as an element of the truth that it discloses. As with spoken language, the languages of art fall short of a perfect merging of horizons, but the greatest artistic achievements let us feel the weight of this insufficiency as a dimension of what the work itself conveys. And so the most piercing beauty is also poignant, an effect produced and enhanced by the sense we have of its fragility and by the fact that it points beyond itself, offering the promise of some further, fuller satisfaction. In the 13th century, Thomas Aquinas argued that beautiful things give us a glimpse of an absolute beauty that we never apprehend directly.[22] Centuries earlier, Augustine of Hippo stated that a poem should be read in such a fashion that it enters into a reader's life, where its particular beauty encourages the reader to go on seeking fulfillment beyond the limits of speech and time.[23] Jacques Lacan held Augustine in high esteem, proclaiming that linguists "have taken fifteen centuries to rediscover, like a sun which has arisen anew, like a dawn that is breaking, ideas which are already set out in Augustine's text, which is one of the most glorious one could read".[24] Such high praise is explained partly by the fact that Lacan found in Augustine a version of his own preoccupation with the juncture between language and desire. But whereas Aquinas and Augustine look forward to a fulfilment of desire in the beatific vision after death, Lacan holds that the gap between desire and language ends when death extinguishes the gap itself. Meanwhile, as long as we are alive, desire is perpetually reproduced in our pursuit of the imagined unattainable wholeness that awakens desire in the first place.

Miguel de Unamuno reflects likewise on the uneasy connections between death, beauty, and unsatisfied desire when he describes beauty as "simply the temporal consolation that compassion seeks. A tragic consolation! And the supreme beauty is that of tragedy".[25] We will return to the topic of tragedy in Chapter 4. Meanwhile, in investing the aesthetic with an exigent moral dimension, Unamuno stands with Gadamer, as well as with other strong interpreters such as Rilke,[26] who claims that the beautiful brings us to the edge of terror, and Wallace Stevens, for whom "death is the mother of beauty".[27] Byung-Chul Han notes that these kinds of strong interpretation are largely missing from the predominantly consumerist, feel-good, mindlessly positive culture of distraction to which we are habituated and in which, mainly to serve commercial interests, the prettified and superficially pleasing are passed off as beautiful.[28] But there is no encounter, no dialogue with those prettified images in which there is no strange otherness, no tragic sense of life, no sense of how our own imperfections meet with the imperfections of the other who is both like and unlike us, whom we can never come to know fully but in and through whom, by way of dialogical encounter, we can happen upon new disclosures, new moments of recognition, discovery, and understanding. In art, such moments are made possible by way of an exchange that, as Gadamer says, remains fundamentally dialogical, shaped by an interplay between participation and imperfection. And so we might say (bowdlerizing Oscar Wilde) that dialogue does indeed imitate art.

Bakhtin: space, time, and transgression

The other major 20th-century thinker who is centrally concerned with dialogue is Mikhail Bakhtin (1895–1975).[29] Like Gadamer, Bakhtin emphasizes that the self is fashioned through personal relationships within specific historical and cultural situations, and as users of language we are always already the bearers of modes of thought that belong to the culture at large. Also, because our horizons are limited, the process of self-fashioning, for Bakhtin and Gadamer alike, remains open and unfinished.

Bakhtin's word for the multiplicity of unfinished dialogues that constitute the open-ended human quest for stability and meaning is

"heteroglossia", and when heteroglossia is reproduced in literature –
supremely, for Bakhtin, in Dostoyevsky – it is "polyphony". That is, in
a Dostoyevsky novel we encounter a "polyphonic" variety of voices
and characters, none of which is simply identifiable with the author.
Also, for Bakhtin (as for Gadamer), art is fundamentally dialogical,
and both men share the same broad intuitions about the interconnections among art, truth, and the search for meaning. But
Bakhtin also is distinctive because of the emphasis he places on two
aspects of dialogue that are especially pertinent to the present study:
the *interdependency between self and other* and *transgression*.

For Bakhtin, only "through the other" does one develop a sense
of "one's self", and as Michael Holquist[30] explains, for Bakhtin the
relationship between "I" and "other" is always asymmetrical. This is
so because we experience ourselves as a work in progress, fraught with
uncertainties even as we strive to shape our lives meaningfully. In
contrast to our own sense of being perpetually unfinished – provisional,
as it were – we tend to attribute to others a more defined identity than
we feel we ourselves possess. One reason for this is that the other has a
position in space that I can observe more clearly than I observe my own
body within which I dwell and which I experience as vulnerable and
unpredictable. Consequently, I am aware of having to override my
insecure and unstable perceptions and judgements in order to present
myself confidently to others. In a similar way, the other's time often
seems to me the measure of a particular narrative continuity. By contrast, my own experience of time is variable, confusingly laminated, and
discontinuous. And so, as Holquist says, whatever sense of personal
stability I have develops from my initial misrecognitions of the other as
more stable and unified than I myself. Yet paradoxically, only through
encountering the values that I see represented in others can I undertake
my own self-fashioning. As Holquist explains, this is so because "only
the other's categories will let me be an object for my own perception".[31]
Eventually, I might indeed discover that the other in fact is not so self-
contained as I imagined, and that the values to which we both aspire
are for the other also frequently riven by contradictions and complexities. In that case, our thinking might evolve dialogically, through
a process of mutual exchange and adaptation, evaluation and re-
evaluation. Consequently, my discovery that I have misrecognized the
other's actual experience need not diminish my interest in the values
that I took the other to represent, and might even increase my desire to
pursue them as worthwhile ideals. And so the close connection between
misrecognition and desire brings us again into territory that is familiar
to readers of Jacques Lacan.

Bakhtin does not deal with desire in Lacan's broadly Freudian sense, but in his fascination with the carnivalesque[32] he shows, much as Lacan also does, how closely bound up language is with the body's irrational urgencies. For Bakhtin, in contrast to the high degree of finish and sense of order characteristic of classical art, the "grotesque realism" of a writer such as Rabelais thrusts at us the body's rudeness, excesses, teeming multiplicity, excrescences, orifices, and deformities – all of which transgress against accepted norms of decency and decorum. As a festival of misrule, the carnival likewise turns prevailing social norms upside down, and this can be liberating, a safety valve releasing the pressures built up by social conformity. In turn, the licensing of carnivals as a strategy for containing social unrest reminds us that there are limits to how much liberation is ever officially permissible.[33]

For Bakhtin, the carnivalesque and its equivalent literary mode, grotesque realism, constitute a style of thinking and engaging with others that he finds also in dialogue, which is likewise open-ended, transgressive, and unpredictable. As Plato argues in the *Symposium*, philosophy is driven by unsatisfied desire (eros), and Plato's dialogues focus throughout on the unruly and transgressive figure of Socrates (who was remarkable, so it seems, for his carnivalesque physical uncomeliness). Also, Plato's great adventure in ideas occurred at the same time as the efflorescence of Greek drama in the City Dionysia, the festival honoring Dionysus, who was an outsider to Athens – a transgressor and a subverter whose worship, as Connor says, "tumbles into carnival and carnival inverts, temporarily, the norms and practices of aristocratic society",[34] while simultaneously pointing the way to new spaces for communication, news ways of thinking, new possibilities for community. In Chapter 5, I will deal further with connections between Plato's dialogues and dramatic spectacle. For now, suffice it to say that the carnivalesque elements of Greek drama and the transgressions of Socrates (which cost him his life, after all) are part of a process by which discourse was being reshaped in new and provocative ways, pitching us into unanticipated ambiguities and contradictions that are the seedbed also of a tragic sense of life, and yet opening upon new vistas of understanding, new possibilities for exploration and communion through the open-ended encounter of ideas. Perhaps, as Unamuno says, the profoundest beauty is that of tragedy, but an analogous aesthetic power in Plato's dialogues (which are never quite divorced from a tragic sense of life) also redirects desire toward new, visionary modes of understanding while returning us always to our ineradicable shortcomings and unquenchable longings.

Bakhtin's insights into the immanence of the other in the self are helpful for the purposes of the present chapter because of how they connect dialogue to a misrecognition of the other's space and time. In so doing, Bakhtin fills out Gadamer's ideas about prejudgement and the fusion of horizons by introducing misrecognition directly – even dramatically – into the process itself of the dialogical exchange, and in this he complements a similar emphasis on misrecognition in Lacan. For Bakhtin, dialogue also is transgressive, a risk-taking venture, and it is helpful to acknowledge that self-fashioning – the work in progress that we are – is not for the fainthearted, and not without peril. Dialogue has its own challenges, its own hazards.

Sir Launcelot misrecognized

In conclusion, a literary example can provide a sense of the complex interweave of misrecognition, prejudgement, desire, transgression, and the tragic sense of life through a mimetic representation of experience such as art offers, and with which we engage dialogically, as Bakhtin and Gadamer explain.

In Book XIX, 10–12, of *Le Morte d'Arthur*,[35] Sir Thomas Malory describes the healing of Sir Urré, a Hungarian knight whose wounds cannot be cured until "the best knight of the world" attends to them. Sir Urré travels widely in search of help, and appears at last in King Arthur's court, where a "hundred knights and ten searched Sir Urré's wounds", but to no avail. Sir Launcelot alone is absent, and Arthur waits impatiently for his return. But when Launcelot hears about the task assigned to him, he tries to avoid it because he knows that he is not the best knight in the world. He has seduced Guinevere, Arthur's wife, a fact of which Arthur is unaware, and so at last Arthur has to order the reluctant Launcelot to search Sir Urré's wounds. Launcelot prays to the Holy Trinity to "give power to heal this sick knight", then adding, "good Lord, never of myself". Then, through Launcelot's intervention, Sir Urré indeed is cured and everyone gives thanks, but "ever Sir Launcelot wept as he had been a child that had been beaten".

This is an arresting and moving little episode in the long saga of the *Morte d'Arthur*, and much of its effect depends on that last line when Launcelot weeps like a beaten child. What has he realized that breaks through his knightly prowess, causing him to ignore the esteem in which he is held, especially at that moment, by the admiring court, as he is thrown back instead on the pain of a child reliving the hurt of an early, helpless grief and separation? It is almost as if Sir Launcelot has been punished just as thoroughly as Sir Urré has been cured, but no one except the reader understands that. Perhaps the knights see Launcelot's tears as expressing relief or gratitude – Malory does not say, and takes care to ensure instead that the reader has more information about the scene than the participants. Malory, after all, provides the comparison to the beaten child, and there is no indication that anyone else (including Launcelot) sees things that way. And so Malory, who rarely uses similes, chooses now to do so in order to produce the single emotional charge that transfigures the entire episode.

To grasp something of the complexity of the writing, here – which, as usual in Malory, can seem deceptively simple – it helps to look first at what is going on among the characters, and then at the reader's relationship with the text, even though these two aspects of the reading process are not entirely separable.

At the beginning of the episode, the king and courtiers accept that Sir Urré can be cured, and this is the frame of reference – the "repertoire", as Wolfgang Iser would say – that we accept so that the story can move forward. Much of what follows depends then on the different points of view of the king, Launcelot, and the courtiers. For his part, the king is confident about Launcelot's virtue: Arthur's most admired knight must surely be "the best". But as we see, Launcelot's prejudgement of the situation is quite different because he knows that his integrity is compromised and that Arthur is seriously mistaken in thinking him virtuous. Then, ironically, the king's prejudgement of Launcelot is confirmed rather than corrected when the cure occurs, and Launcelot learns that he in fact is the one who has misread the situation by making false assumptions about God's mercy. For the courtiers and the king alike, presumably, the cure is a sign that God's grace has co-operated with Launcelot's virtue, and these admiring observers are far from disabused of their idealizing opinions. When Launcelot kneels and prays before the cure occurs, the courtiers do not hear the words that he speaks secretly to himself, but they no doubt see a gesture of humility, confirmed by Launcelot's tears after the cure is effected.

These interactions among the characters are therefore shaped by different prejudgements and expectations that in turn give rise to misrecognitions, ranging from the personal (Arthur) to the social (the court) and cosmic (the overarching mystery of God's providence). One effect of this expanding pattern is to extend the narrative toward the universal, but then the outwardly expanding movement also throws Launcelot's singular, private grief and remorse all the more sharply into relief. Furthermore, the reader's frame of reference is broader than that of the courtly participants because the reader knows about Launcelot's guilty secret, and is Malory's confidant in a way that the others are not. And so the reader is well positioned to understand the ironies of misrecognition that leave Launcelot so painfully alone. As is perennially the case, Launcelot's relationship with Guinivere was born out of desire, the imagined promise of a union that, as Lacan says, would heal the trauma of childhood separation into the symbolic, where desire is engendered. Yet the answer to Launcelot's prayer in the healing of Sir Urré makes it all the more clear both to Launcelot and to us that he is far from healed by his relationship with Guinevere, as he experiences again the full weight and grief of the child's hurt and isolation. And so the episode taps down into the deepest sources where separation, unfulfillable desire, longing, and grief are bound inextricably together in a complex imbroglio that art is uniquely ordered to show in an emotionally engaging manner, by means of which we might discover something new and of value about our relationship with the world and others.

Finally, throughout the Sir Urré episode, the designs of divine providence remain mysterious, and the "appalling – strangeness of the mercy of God" (as one of Graham Greene's characters says)[36] sets Launcelot's personal experience against the unfathomable ground that Lacan refers to as the Real and Rilke describes as the terrifying dimension without which beauty is trivial or merely ornamental. And so it does not do to sentimentalize. Arthur remains deceived, and his confidence and pride in Launcelot make Launcelot's predicament all the more problematic. Also, as the reader knows but the participants in the story do not, the seeds of the tragic destruction of Camelot are already sown by Launcelot's betrayal of his king.

As Gadamer says, our encounter with art is dialogical, and our personal horizons interact unpredictably with the complexities, challenges, and revelations offered by the work before us. The Sir Urré episode shows how this is so, as we engage with the several dimensions of the scene in which variously fused horizons, misrecognitions, and prejudgements reach out to include us in the rich complexities (and perplexities) with which the story deals. And although my remarks about Malory draw on analytical tools that are products of the modern era and not the Middle Ages, it is worth emphasizing, as I have argued in Chapter 2, that modern analytical language does not diminish the effectiveness of earlier forms of narrative, metaphor, symbolism, and myth in communicating powerful insights about our condition. To the contrary, these insights can be more powerfully experienced by being made more fully conscious through an appropriately sensitive conceptual investigation.

In this chapter, I have suggested that we participate in this kind of investigation as the bearers of prejudgements that commit us to certain misrecognitions which also stabilize our world and enable us to act purposefully. By entering into dialogue, we engage then in a process whereby mutual enquiry into what we hold to be the case is a means of discovering more adequate ways of thinking and understanding. There is no final word and no fully achieved understanding, but the acknowledgement of imperfection is itself a guarantor that the dialogical spirit stays alive, fueled as it is by desire. As Plato says, all genuine philosophy is eros translated into thinking.[37] And yet eros remains always to some degree unfulfilled, however radiant the moments of discovery, revelation, and beauty encountered along the way, registering a fragile if exigent protest: "How with this rage shall beauty hold a plea, /Whose action is no stronger than a flower?"[37]

Notes

1 Thomas Browne, *Religio Medici*, in *The Prose of Sir Thomas Browne*, ed. Norman Endicott (New York: New York University Press, 1968), p. 73.

2 See Alain Badiou, *I Know There Are So Many of You*, trans. Susan Spitzer (Medford, MA: Polity Press, 2019), pp. 1 and 6, describing some "essential banalities, of the kind that must never be forgotten", among them "this basic unity, this biological and mental Same". See also, Terry Eagleton, *Why Marx Was Right* (New Haven and London: Yale University Press, 2011), pp. 80 ff.

3 There is a great variety of advocacy groups, social justice organizations, and human-rights organizations, among many other similar initiatives, as a brief look at the website Activist Facts confirms. For a sampling of approaches to this complex phenomenon, see William Kaplan, *Why Dissent Matters: Because Some People See things the Rest of Us Miss* (Montreal: McGill-Queen's University Press, 2017); Clive Hamilton and Sarah Madison, *Silencing Dissent. How the Australian Government Is Controlling Public Opinion and Stifling Debate* (New South Wales: Allen and Unwin, 2007); Milton Glazer, Mirko Ilic, Steven Heller, and Tony Kushner, *The Design of Dissent, Expanded Edition: Greed, Nationalism, Alternative Facts, and the Resistance* (Beverly, MA: Quarto, 2017).

4 *I Know There So Many of You*, p. 33.

5 See *Immanuel Kant's Critique of Pure Reason*, trans. Norman Kemp Smith (New York: St. Martin's Press, 1965), p. 183.

6 "Biographia Litteraria." *The Complete Works of Samuel Taylor Coleridge*, ed. Professor Shedd (New York: Harper, 1868), III, p. 363.

7 Jacques Lacan, *The Four Fundamental Concepts of Psycho-Analysis*, ed. Jacques-Alain Miller, trans. Alan Sheridan (New York: Norton, 1978), p. 26. The following broad account of Lacan's thinking draws also on *The Seminar of Jacques Lacan*, ed. Jacques-Alain Miller, Books I and II, trans. John Forrester and Sylvana Tomaselli (New York: Norton, 1988); *Écrits: a*

Selection, trans. Alan Sheridan (London: Tavistock, 1977); *The Language of the Self. The Function of Language in Psychoanalysis*, trans. Anthony Wilden (Baltimore: Johns Hopkins University Press, 1968); Ellie Ragland Sullivan, *Jacques Lacan and the Philosophy of Psychoanalysis* (Urbana and Chicago: University of Illinois Press, 1986).

8 The following summary of Hans-Georg Gadamer draws on *Truth and Method*, trans. and rev. Joel Weinsheimer and Donald G. Marshall (London: Bloomsbury, 1989); *Dialogue and Dialectic: Eight Hermeneutical Studies on Plato*, trans. P. Christopher Smith (New Haven: Yale Univ. Press, 1980); *Relevance of the Beautiful and Other Essays*, ed. Robert Bernasconi (Cambridge: Cambridge Univ. Press, 1986); *Philosophical Hermeneutics*, trans. and ed. David E. Linge (Berkeley: Univ. of California Press, 1976). Useful commentaries are provided by Donatella Di Cesare, *Gadamer. A Philosophical Portrait*, trans. Niall Keane (Bloomington: Indiana Univ. Press, 2007); Jean Grondin, *The Philosophy of Gadamer*, trans. Kathryn Plant (Montreal: McGill-Queen's Univ. Press, 2003); *The Philosophy of Hans-Georg Gadamer*, ed. Lewis Edwin Hahn (Illinois: Open Court, 1997).

9 See, for instance, "Martin Heidegger and Marburg Theology (1964)", and "Heidegger and the Language of Metaphysics (1967)", in *Philosophical Hermeneutics*, trans. and ed. David E. Linge. pp. 198 ff. and 229 ff.

10 Di Cesare, *Gadamer. A Philosophical Portrait*, p. 158, citing Gadamer's *Ästhetik und Poetik I: Kunst als Aussage*, in *Gesammelte Werke*, vol. 8 (Tubingen: J.C.B. Mohr, 1993), p. 369.

11 Merlin Donald, *Origins of the Modern Mind. Three Stages in the Evolution of Culture and Cognition* (Cambridge, MA: Harvard Univ. Press, 1993; first published, 1991), p. 234.

12 David Bohm, *On Dialogue* (London: Routledge, 2013). On language belonging to the whole culture, see pp. 14, 51, 71; on participatory consciousness, see pp. 26, 47, 84; on embodied skill, see pp. 52, 74, 179.

13 Michael Polanyi, *Personal Knowledge. Towards a Post-Critical Philosophy* (New York: Harper Torchbooks, 1964; first published, 1958), p. 64. David Bohm cites Polanyi: see *On Dialogue*, p. 52.

14 Maurice Merleau-Ponty, *Signs*, trans. Richard C. McCleary (Evanston, Ill: Northwestern Univ. Press, 1964; first published, 1960), p. 42.

15 See *Truth and Method*, pp. 282 ff., 288 ff.

16 See *Truth and Method*, pp. 317, 350, 600 ff.

17 Di Cesare, *Gadamer, A Philosophical Portrait*, p. 160, points out that friendship was "the guiding thread that Gadamer followed from the beginning to the end of his path of thought". See p. 174 note 44.

18 Grandin, *The Philosophy of Gadamer*, p. 129, citing "The Limits of Language" (1985), *Gesammelte Werke*, 8, 361.

19 Henry Vaughan (1622–95), "Cock-crowing".

20 The following summary draws on *Truth and Method*, Part One, "The Question of Truth as it Emerges in the Experience of Art"; "Aesthetics and Hermeneutics", in *Philosophical Hermeneutics*, pp. 95–104; "The Relevance of the Beautiful", in *The Relevance of the Beautiful and Other Essays*, trans. Nicholas Walker, edited with an Introduction by Robert Bernasconi (Cambridge: Cambridge University Press, 1986).

21 For an account of Aquinas on art and beauty, see Jacques Maritain, *Art and Scholasticism. With Other Essays*, trans. J. F. Scanlon (London: Sheed and Ward, 1930), pp. 31 ff.

22 Augustine of Hippo, *Confessions*, XI, 8; XII, 12; XIII, 8.

23 Jacques Lacan, *The Seminar, Book I: Freud's Papers on Technique* (1953–1954) (New York: Norton), p. 249.

24 Miguel de Unamuno, *Tragic Sense of Life*, trans. J. E. Crawford Flitch (New York: Dover, 1954; first published, 1921), p. 203.

25 Rainer Maria Rilke, *Duino Elegies*, trans. Stephen Mitchell (London: Vintage, 2009), p. 3.

26 Wallace Stevens, "Sunday Morning", *The Collected Poems* (New York: Vintage, 1954), pp. 71 ff.

27 Byung-Chul Han, *Saving Beauty*, trans. Daniel Steuer (Cambridge: Polity, 2018), pp. 48–49, *et passim*.

28 The following summary of Mikhail Bakhtin draws on *Problems of Dostoevsky's Poetics*, ed. and trans. Caryl Emerson, introduction by Wayne C. Booth (Minneapolis: Univ. of Minnesota Press, 1984); *Dialogic Imagination. Four Essays by M.M. Bakhtin*, ed. Michael Holquist, trans. Caryl Emerson and Michael Holquist (Austin: Univ. of Texas Press, 1981); *Rabelais and His World*, trans. Helene Iswolsky (Cambridge, MA: MIT Press, 1968).

29 Michael Holquist, *Dialogism: Bakhtin and His World* (London: Routledge, 1990), p. 19. The following paragraphs summarize Holquist's helpful account and interpretation of Bakhtin, especially on space, time, and the other.

30 See Holquist, *Dialogism*, p. 28.

31 See especially *Rabelais and His World*.

32 See Peter Stallybrass and Allon White, *The Politics and Poetics of Transgression* (London: Methuen, 1986), p. 19.

33 W. Robert Connor, "Civil Society, Dionysiac Festival, and the Athenian Democracy", in *Dēmokratia: A Conversation on Democracies, Ancient and Modern*, ed. Josiah Ober and Charles Hedrick (Princeton: Princeton Univ. Press, 1996), p. 222, cited in Bellah, *Religion in Human Evolution*, p. 351.

34 The following citations are from Sir Thomas Malory, *Le Morte D'Arthur*, 2 vols., ed. Janet Cowen, with an introduction by John Lawlor (Harmondsworth: Penguin, 1969), vol. 2, pp. 446–453.

35 Graham Greene, *Brighton Rock*, part 7, 11.

36 See *Symposium*, 203 c.

37 William Shakespeare, Sonnet 65.

4 On the side of the sunflowers

The boundaries of reason and desire

Desire, then, is desire for the other who is never fully accessible, and the always further-reaching of desire is quenched only when the body dies. Confronted by the prospect of merely a dead end, those who are theologically inclined look to some greater fulfillment in an afterlife. In so doing, they frequently insist also that the soul is incomplete – indeed, unthinkable – without a body. That is, if the immortal soul is to find itself fulfilled in the vision of God, the body must somehow continue, because without it we are not ourselves.

The wellspring of this hopeful conviction is simply that we want to go on living, despite the fact that reason does not do well in explaining how such a thing might happen, given that we die. Thomas Aquinas,[1] as always the dauntless reasoner, remains almost amazingly unflinching when he considers how deceased human embryos are to appear on the Last Day. If, say, a cannibal eats only human flesh and then has a child who also eats only human flesh, how are the resurrected bodies of the well-fed child and its human food chain to be reconstituted? What is to become of our hair and nail clippings? What age will we be on the Last Day, and will bodily deformities be repaired? The mind recoils from such embarrassingly materialized absurdities, but the desire to live on after death while somehow maintaining a personal identity goes on encouraging reason to try to swallow one such camel after another. And so among people in general, across the globe and throughout history, the desire to survive death remains, let us say, unreasonably persistent. Even the Buddha, who insists on anatta, or the nonexistence of a self, consigns the problem of our status after death to the realm of an "undecided point". He does so on the grounds that he prefers not to side with either the ascetic annihilationists or the Brahmin eternalists, and so he leaves the question decently up in the air.[2] As Lao-tzu reminds us, to be alive is to suffer,[3] and yet ironically, we suffer not least because of our persistent desire for fulfillment beyond suffering.

As Bakhtin argues, in dialogue we are also caught up in the perpetual discontent of an unfinalizable search that carries us along the chains and through the networks of signification in search of meaning, understanding, and communion as we contend with circumstances we did not choose at birth and with which we have to go on grappling until we die. As Bakhtin says, within these constraints that, perplexingly, excite desire even as they prevent its fulfillment, dialogue is our most effective means for finding directions out. In a perceptive book on the topic, Dmitri Nikulin concludes that dialogue is nothing more or less than "the art of being human",[4] and like Gadamer, he insists on the analogy between dialogue and art on the grounds that both are intersubjective experiences entailing a decentering of the ego and an openness to encounter and to a transfiguration of the familiar. As with art in general, dialogue engages with the whole range of registers and modes of verbal, mimetic, and somatic exchange that have accompanied our emergence as a species, as I have suggested in Chapter 2. But we are not to forget that words can be dangerous and we can be altogether too clever for our own good. The declaration of the Delphic Oracle, "know thyself", is, after all, not just an invitation to introspection; it is an injunction also to recognize one's limits, and it contains a warning about overstepping. Although we desire power and immortality, there are limits to what we can know and achieve. And so Odysseus's success in getting home to Ithaca lay not least in the fact that, by and large, he knew his place in relation to the fickle but powerful gods and he did not unduly tempt their retribution.

A few centuries after the Greek epics were written down, the tragic drama of fifth-century Athens focused especially on the processes of retribution that Odysseus contrived to avoid, and that the dramatists present as so devastating as to force us to question whatever comforting notions we might have about divine justice, whether in this life or any other. Interestingly, as I mentioned in Chapter 3, this remarkable exploration occurred under the influence of the boundary-breaking Dionysius, at whose festival the tragedies were performed. As Bellah[5] explains, the growth of the Dionysiac cult in fifth-century Greece contributed to the development of Athenian democracy because the transgressive, irreverent Dionysiac spirit opened up new spaces for discussion by raising radical questions about justice, authority, and human autonomy, while highlighting the uncomfortable problem of undeserved, disproportionate human suffering. But as

Nietzsche reminds us, Dionysiac energy is also terrifying, and in the Greek tragedies Dionysius is locked in an unresolved – and un-resolvable – struggle with Apollo, whose rule of reason, however illusory (for Nietzsche, we need to remember, Apollo is a dreamer), is indispensable for the prevention of total chaos. As an "Apollonian embodiment of Dionysiac insight and powers", the tragic drama takes its life from the conflict between these two principles.[6] That is, without Apollo, there would be no language to give form to the inarticulate fury and chaos of the Dionysiac, but without Dionysus there would be no creativity. As always, the further-reaching of a desire to affirm life and defeat death demands gratification, even as reason declares that there are limits, and transgression brings down the often dispropor-tionate and pitiless anger of the gods. This is the core of tragedy, from which we do not stand far removed, negotiating, as we always are, the boundaries between reason and desire. Simply put, the aspiration to go on living contradicts the knowledge that we die, and this is the linchpin of Unamuno's understanding of the tragic view of life.

Abject silences

I will return by and by to Nietzsche and Dionysus, but in order to provide a frame of reference for a further consideration of the chal-lenges and insights offered by tragedy in relation to dialogue, I want now to consider two kinds of limits within which dialogue is con-strained to take place, and beyond which language (tragically) cannot reach. The first draws on what is sometimes called the "perennial philosophy" – that is, the common core of experience and insight transcending doctrinal and cultural differences in the world's main religious traditions. One central theme in the literature of the perennial philosophy is that people can have direct experiences of the trans-cendent, and the way toward such experiences lies through the relin-quishment of the ego and the giving over of self-interest in becoming open to the One, Tao, God, Brahman, nirvana. Of the experience itself of union, or fusion, or transcendent meaning, nothing can be said except imperfectly and indirectly. And so St. Teresa of Avila writes that "there is no sense of anything, only fruition, without under-standing what that is the fruition of which is granted. It is understood that the fruition is of a certain good containing in itself all good to-gether at once; but this good is not comprehended".[7] Lao-tzu calls attention to the insufficiency of the means of communication when he assures us that "the Tao that can be told is not the eternal Tao. /The name that can be named is not the eternal name".[8] Along similar lines,

The Diamond Sutra tells us, "The Tathāgata [Buddha] has no for-mulated teaching to enunciate. Wherefore? Because the Tathāgata has said that truth is uncontainable and inexpressible. It neither is nor is not".[9] St. Bernard of Clairvaux pushes the limits of taste (if I can be allowed the pun) as well as the limits of language in describing mystical experience as a sort of mutual cannibalism: "I am masticated when I am reproved; I am swallowed when I am instructed", for "were I to feed on Him whilst He did not feed on me, He, just as now, would appear to be in me, yet I should not truly be in Him". The obtrusive materiality of Bernard's comparison causes us to recoil from the literal sense towards its inexpressible referent – as he no doubt intends – and in so doing we are reminded that our corporeality cannot be jettisoned but sticks around, getting in the way, like language itself, even when it tries to point beyond itself. As with the "fullness" to which Teresa points, Bernard's experience exceeds the reach of words because it carries more significance than language can bear. As St. John of the Cross writes, the "loftiest wisdom" can only be received "in a spirit that is silent" and detached from "discursive knowledge".[10]

Claims to having such special, ineffable experiences provoke us to ask whether or not the people making such claims are deluded, and the standard response is that a person who is observed to be morally sound and otherwise dependable would probably not indulge in out-landish fabrication. As Æ (George Russell) assures us, a vision must be testable in its consequences, and we do best to ignore a "religion which does not cry out: 'I am today verifiable as that water wets or that fire burns'".[11] In similar fashion, William of Saint-Thierry writes that "in this question of seeing God", "it seems to me that there is more value in one's manner of living than in his manner of speaking".[12] Just so, the silent meditation in which the Buddha became enlightened was a preface to his lifelong dedication to instructing others, and the fact that he lived according to his precepts might incline us to consider that his special private experience was not merely a delusion.

One further point insisted upon by the perennial philosophy is that experiences of union with the encompassing mystery, the source of "original being" (as Taoism says), are followed by a return to the world of ordinary human discourse, which is to be re-engaged with the same selflessness as the ineffable experience required as its precondi-tion. The problems of suffering and injustice remain then to be en-countered in our ordinary world, and the value of the special experiences that the saints and mystics describe informs their sub-sequent moral relationships, the quality of their dialogue with others – as immediate as fire and water, as Æ says.

But there is another kind of silence, also setting a limit beyond which dialogue cannot take us. This is the silence of abjection, in which the other is deprived of speech and given no opportunity to answer back. Simone Weil argues that in such a situation both the oppressor and the oppressed are dehumanized, and she writes of the rule of force that "its power of converting a man into a thing is a double one, and in its application double-edged. To the same degree, though in different fashions, those who use it and those who endure it are turned to stone".[13] That is, the diminishment of the oppressor and the oppressed is reciprocal, however unequal the balance of power. But then also, as history keeps showing us, the balance of power might shift and today's vanquished become tomorrow's victors, fueled by grievance and all too willing to pay back with a vengeance in the same coin as was paid out to them. Warfare, oppression, enslavement keep us going in a perpetual circle of recrimination, as they have always done, and if the common insights of the world's religions are referred to as the "perennial philosophy", so also there is a "perennial pathology", which we might describe as the way of "downward transcendence", driven by the rule of force and fueled by recrimination and revenge.

A telling example of the pre-emption of dialogue by the rule of force is provided in a perceptive study by Richard Davis of the Troubles in Northern Ireland (roughly from 1969 to 1998). Davis shows how the main opposed paramilitary factions mirrored each other's violent rhetoric and behavior, falling into stereotypical patterns of re-crimination, revenge, and mutual abjection of the other by way of an unconscious "cultural convergence".[14] That is, the opposed groups came to look more and more alike despite the fact that they thought of themselves as implacable enemies, utterly different. As the Northern Ireland poet John Hewitt writes, this mutual hatred is an "iron circle"[15] that can't be broken, because it pre-empts the meeting and exchange whereby enemies might discover in each other some personal dimension that does not fit the stereotype of what is loathed and feared. As always, violence depends on depersonalizing, and especially in the case of political or ethnic violence, the other is silenced and becomes an anonymous representative of a group. Thus, an IRA member explains that in attacking the army and police, "most volunteers got it into their minds that it was the uniform and not the individual that was being shot".[16] The same point is made by the loyalist paramilitary slogan ATD ("any Taig will do"), meaning that any Catholic chosen at random is a suitable target. Ex-IRA member Eamon Collins explains how eventually he came to see that in fact "you can never kill a uniform, you can only kill a person",[17] and

Michael Asher, British former soldier and member of the elite SAS, recalling his experiences in Northern Ireland, writes that the "worship of violence" "prevented us from remembering that the IRA were human beings like us".[18] Commendably, by writing about their change of heart Collins and Asher open a space for better understanding to develop, and this is all very well. But is it enough? What would the victims think if they were not deprived of speech and so utterly silenced? What is the value of insight after the damage is done? These questions arise pressingly also from the heart of tragedy, as we shall see.

For now, I have argued that the silence of transcendence and the silence of abjection both pre-empt dialogue. On the one hand, the saints and mystics return to engage with an imperfect world in light of their ineffable vision. On the other hand, those who have lived by violence return with a message aimed at breaking the entail of the iron circle. Karl Jaspers, who writes well about existential choice, points us towards what he calls the "encompassing", by which he means the unity of all that is and which we affirm by an act of "philosophical faith".[19] The alternative, he says, is nihilism, and life is lived for the most part between these limit conditions (the two silences, as it were) – the affirmation of an encompassing mystery and a nihilistic denial of it. The in-between condition is, I want to suggest, the site of dialogue, the means by which values and meaning are shaped for specific purposes through the trials and errors of a limited self-fashioning.

Still, we cannot live our lives exclusively within the interpersonal sphere of dialogue, and for practical purposes we need to engage with the world of things and objects, the purely informational "It", as Buber says, which includes our objectified relations with others. The dialogical "I-Thou" therefore alternates with the impersonal "I-It",[20] through a continuing interplay between the personal and the instrumental. As we have also seen, extreme objectification leads to violence, the simplest and most efficient instrumental means of dealing with others – which is to say, through control and domination – and we are reminded daily that the totalitarian agents of abjection are far from giving any advantage to the advocates of a dialogical exchange with others for the benefit of all. Furthermore, there is no adequate explanation of the suffering caused by violence, whether moral or natural, that is even close to comforting or convincing. Theology breaks against the problem of evil that it cannot solve, short of quibbling rationalization, and there is plenty of good reason to refuse religious belief even if the recoil of indignation and horror, which any conscionable reflection on the problem of evil produces, in itself expresses an aspiration to something better. In this context, it is helpful to recall William Law's unusual but salutary suggestion that we are saved not because of Jesus's suffering, but despite it.[21] That is, faced with Jesus's abjection, it seems that the least we can do is repudiate his suffering, and here the believer and nonbeliever might share some common ground. And yet it is also all too true that as long as we have the leisure to reflect on such a repudiation, we do not fully share the abject condition for which we express sympathy. Protest is spoken always from within a safe-enough sanctuary, removing us from the full experience of that which we denounce. I will return to this point later in the chapter. For now, let us consider the Gospel story of Jesus's transfiguration, which brings together the main points I have so far been making about the silence of transcendence and the silence of abjection in relation to the boundaries of reason, desire, and language.

Transfiguration and meeting others again

The transfiguration occurs when Jesus takes Peter, James, and John "up into a high mountain", and the three main synoptic accounts (Mark 9:1–35, Matthew 17:1–27, and Luke 9:28–48) tell how the disciples witness Christ's gloriously altered face and body. Jesus then asks his disciples to keep silent about what they have seen "till the Son of Man were risen from the dead" (Mark 9:9, Matthew17:9), a saying that the disciples do not understand.

Later, at the foot of the mountain, Jesus and the disciples are met by a crowd of people, including the father of an epileptic boy. The man asks for his son to be healed and the disciples try to oblige him but fail. Jesus is exasperated by what he declares to be a general condition of faithlessness ("O faithless and perverse generation, how long shall I be with you? How long shall I suffer you?" [Matthew 17:17]), and he performs the cure himself. When the disciples wonder why they were unsuccessful, Jesus says bluntly: "because of your unbelief" (Matthew 17:20). He then predicts his own death and resurrection, and according to Mark, the disciples "understood not" (9:32), but were afraid to ask.

To grasp the broader significance of this sequence of events for the Gospel narratives as a whole, we need to consider the story about curing the blind man at Bethsaida, which occurs directly before the transfiguration. This is the only two-stage miracle in the Gospels, and Jesus begins by spitting on the blind man's eyes but manages only to effect a partial cure. ("I see men as trees, walking" [Mark 8:24] says the man, so graphically, about his fuzzy vision.) On the second attempt, Jesus succeeds, and afterwards asks his disciples, "Whom do men say that I am?" (8:27). "Thou art the Christ" (8:29), Peter tells him. But when Jesus goes on to predict his own death and resurrection, Peter is unable to accept what he is told, and Jesus turns on him so vehemently as to leave little doubt about his displeasure. "Get Thee behind me, Satan", (8:33), he says, and we can only imagine the bewildered Peter's reaction to this excoriating rebuke.

The main point in this troubling exchange is that although Peter identifies Jesus as Christ, he cannot accept the news about Jesus's suffering, and so he fails to understand that the visionary experience on the mountain cannot, without distortion, be separated from the suffering of people in the ordinary world. The transfiguration, about which the disciples are told not to speak, and the muteness of the epileptic boy who "foameth, and gnasheth with his teeth" (Mark 9:18), can therefore represent the silence of transcendence and the silence of abjection as the limits within which effective human discourse and agency occur. Because the disciples do not grasp this point, they are unable to heal the sick. Here, it is important to notice that Jesus does not reason with the disciples or try to explain the suffering with which he contends in others and predicts for himself. Rather, the scandal of suffering is acknowledged for what it is, and we are to accept the full weight of the problem – including the lack of adequate explanation. This is part of what the cross itself means, and the cross in turn brings us to the stony silence of the tomb, against which the resurrection stands as a protest that remains inseparable from the tragic events preceding it. Although the resurrection is intimated by the transfiguration,[22] the disciples who witness the event on the mountain still have a lot to learn about the tragedy of the cross. On the mountain, it is as if speech is silenced in the glorious fullness of the moment, but some kinds of suffering call meaning itself into question, and the disciples' response to the crucifixion was to flee in disarray and confusion – in abjection, as it were. Consequently, tragedy, which thematizes the silencing of dialogue before the unanswerable problem of unjust or disproportionate suffering, requires special attention in connection with whatever claims we might want to make about how meaning is discovered and shared through dialogue.

Tragedy: nothing left to say

For Ovid, tragedy is the highest form of literature, an opinion shared by Milton and Schopenhauer, for whom tragedy is, simply, the "highest poetical achievement", because it represents "the terrible side of life".[23] In the *Poetics,*[24] Aristotle singles out pity and fear as the main emotions that tragedy stimulates in response to the terrible spectacles with which it presents us. In turn, pity and fear are purged by the catharsis that tragedy effects, and which leaves us emptied out, suspended, as it were, in a state of post-traumatic, contemplative silence.

Although Aristotle does not spell it out, there is a correspondence in the *Poetics* between his remarks about pity and about probability, and also about fear and necessity. "Probability" means our acceptance that, within the universe depicted by the play, the events that occur there might well happen. "Necessity" means that we understand how these events, once set in motion, unfold inevitably. Probability is therefore connected to pity, because we can feel some compassionate concern for characters with whose situation we can identity imaginatively, recognizing it as probable. Necessity is connected to fear, because we understand how events and circumstances can unfold in an impersonal manner, regardless of what seems just and deserved. This pitiless and cruel, yet all too probable unfolding is "the terrible side of life" that Schopenhauer says tragedy reveals, and which, according to Aristotle, we experience in a powerfully emotional way as the spectacle reaches into the deep recesses from which fear and pity spring – that is, the primal terrors and their antidote, our primal desire for communion.

Although the *Poetics* is a loose collection of notes, Aristotle identifies some key motifs that have remained central to tragedy as a genre, even though individual tragedies can be very different from each other. For instance, *Antigone, Hamlet, Phèdre*, and *Death of a Salesman* are so unlike that it is not clear how we should describe them all as, somehow, the same. In *The Event of Literature*, Terry Eagleton addresses this question of sameness and difference by recalling how he once held the position that literature has no essence, but changed his mind on the basis that "nominalism is not the only alternative to essentialism".[25] That is, it is false to say that either something has an essence or the words used to describe it are empty. To develop the point, Eagleton refers to Wittgenstein's explanation of games, which, Wittgenstein argues, have no single element in common but are connected through networks of "family resemblances". That is, although games have no essential characteristic, it makes sense to use the word "game", which we understand in different contexts by way of various overlaps and resemblances. Eagleton then applies this "family resemblance" theory to literature – or "literature talk", as he says.

In his remarkable book *Why Does Tragedy Give Pleasure*, A.D. Nuttall[26] also refers to Wittgenstein's theory about games, applying it to tragedy. If we look only at the differences among tragedies, Nuttall suggests, we soon find ourselves in "a universe of windowless, monadic individuals". But it is worth remembering that just as it makes sense to use the word "person" even though "every person we meet is unique" (82), so likewise it makes sense to refer to the individual plays – say, of Sophocles, Shakespeare, Racine, and Miller – as tragedies. Nuttall goes on to suggest that in tragedy "the element of the great person destroyed" is so "insistently repeated, over and over again" (82) that it emerges as a key criterion for the genre, without being definitive. In addition, I would add that in a tragedy the qualities that make the person "great" are, in the specific circumstances that the play presents, the engine of the great person's destruction. By such means, tragedy returns us to the problem of disproportionate suffering that we experience as probable and even – in certain situations in which character and circumstance are fatally combined – inevitable, or necessary. We might say then that tragedy typically confronts us with the problem of disproportionate, unjustified suffering and how it occurs when circumstance and character combine in a fatal constellation of probability and necessity leading to the destruction of a great person, so convincingly depicted as to leave us emotionally drained and silent.

And yet, we might also want to take a step back and ask how fearful are we, really, and how deep does our pity reach? Tragedy, after all, is art, and it engages us within the relatively safe precincts of the dialogical, even as it explores the breaking point at which dialogue is silenced and art itself seems futile. Dr. Johnson[27] correctly points out that the pleasure we take in tragedy depends on the fact that we know it is a fiction that insulates us from the full force of the events being depicted. A spectator who thinks that Gloucester's eyes are actually gouged out and trampled on stage is going to feel different from a spectator who knows that *King Lear* is a play and the actor is unharmed. And just as the fiction keeps us at a distance, so also the formal means of expression – the conventions of the genre, the playwright's strategies, and so on – are central to the aesthetic experience as distinct from actual life.

Still, neither is tragedy just a formal description of the events it depicts. The emotions it evokes are real even if they are kept safely enough at bay. As Gadamer says, aesthetic experience takes us out of the everyday but also maintains a continuity with everyday concerns, and the paradoxical status of art in general is that it does not simply reproduce the actual world nor can it be entirely separated from it. Wolfgang Iser[28] confirms Gadamer's point by arguing that fiction is a product of imagination but also tells us about reality, showing us the familiar world in a new light and inviting us to transform ourselves accordingly. This process of engagement and transformation depends, in turn, on the boundaries between fictive and real, subject and object, self and other being permeable.

The facts that boundaries are not defined and audience (or reader) response is not uniform can remind us in turn that tragedy typically confronts us with the analogously undecidable, overarching riddle of the meaning of life itself. And insofar as tragedy challenges us in this way, its disturbing power exceeds the formal means of expression, which are insufficient to the urgency of the questions raised, so that, as Hamlet says, "the rest is silence". Interestingly, Dr. Johnson confesses that he could not bear to reread *King Lear* (until he had to do so in order to edit it) because he found it too distressing.[29] And so his reassurance that events represented in a drama are fictional and we are therefore able to enjoy the play seems not to have worked in his own case, as far as *King Lear* is concerned. The imaginative power of the representation simply broke across the boundaries of the containing form, and theatrical convention failed to provide sufficient protection from the terrifying vision that *King Lear* presents. At the beginning of Western speculation about the function of art in society, Plato already worried that the emotions stirred up by poetry could be too unruly to be contained, and one recommendation in the *Republic* is simply to banish the poets (with some exceptions). As Nuttall says, Plato's student, Aristotle, stays closer to his teacher on this topic than is often realized, but instead of banishing the poets, he recommends banishing the harmful emotions – which is to say, purging them by a process that is not exactly pleasant and that leaves us feeling emptied out.

The facts that the boundaries between audience and theatrical performance are unstable, and that tragedy presents challenges that break through conventional boundaries, help also to explain why the ancient Greek drama was performed at festivals for Dionysus.[30] As an outsider to Greece, Dionysus was already a boundary-breaker, a troublemaker whose spirit of misrule was disruptive and destabilizing. And yet, as I have pointed out, the chaotic, unpredictable Dionysiac energy opened up new spaces, discovering new possibilities and producing new, discomfiting questions and insights for discussion in the public sphere. The extant tragedies from the period (they are all from the fifth century) with one exception do not deal with Dionysus directly, a fact which suggests that they were performed instead under the influence of the Dionysiac spirit, with which, as Nietzsche clearly saw, the Apollonian rational order inevitably contends. As I also mentioned earlier in this chapter, for Nietzsche, Dionysus is terrifying, and life lived entirely under the rule of Dionysus would be unbearable. A degree of Apollonian order is necessary, and, consequently, for Nietzsche, when the hero is at last consumed by the terrifying impersonality of the Dionysiac realm, "like a mighty titan", he "shoulders the whole Dionysiac world and removes the burden from us",[31] restoring us, however shaken, to the illusory order of the everyday. Just as in the Gospels the cross is the sign against which signification itself breaks, so in tragedy our hopes and desires for justice break against the terrifying, Dionysiac fatality with which the drama confronts us. Faced with this realization, Schopenhauer argued that in tragedy the "noblest men" are exemplary because they are resigned to the point where they "freely and joyfully surrender life itself".[32] Schopenhauer's pessimism is, as usual, in the ascendant here, except for that unexpected "joyfully" – though we might wonder what exactly is so joyful. Yeats, drawing on Nietzsche, declares a similar manic abandonment to "tragic joy",[33] and in light of these surprising affirmations spoken out of the heart of the terrible, we might ask if, in tragedy, the silence of abjection and the failure of dialogue are to have the last word. The tragedy that for me addresses these questions most powerfully and disturbingly, to the point of calling the discourse (or dialogue) of the play itself into question, is Shakespeare's *King Lear*.

King Lear: dialogue on empty

As is often noted, *King Lear*[34] begins in the manner almost of a fairy tale, with the aged Lear dividing up his kingdom. In the presence of his assembled court, he asks his three daughters to express their love for him to demonstrate that they deserve their portion of the inheritance. The two older daughters, Goneril and Regan, deliver suitably hyperbolic and flattering speeches, but the youngest, Cordelia, refuses to play Lear's game and says nothing. The king is offended, embarrassed, discomposed, and coaxes her to respond in a manner more in keeping with his intentions. But Cordelia remains uncompliant, tongue-tied because of her genuine love for her father, even though she also demonstrates some obduracy, skirting perhaps on what we might today identify as something like teenage petulance. Lear then becomes so angry that he disinherits her, and to compound her humiliation he advises her suitors that they will receive no dowry because "her price is fallen" (I, 1, 197). The King of France accepts Cordelia anyway, and she departs with him.

Goneril and Regan soon behave like the standard evil sisters that they are, and as soon as they have money and power, they turn against their father, who, when he recognizes his mistake, is driven to madness by the excess of his own rage and remorse. As the play develops, whatever fairy-tale atmosphere was evoked by the opening scenes is replaced by the all too immediate impress of a cruelly harsh realism.

A subplot paralleling the main story of Lear and his three daughters deals with the Duke of Gloucester and his two sons, one of whom, Edmund, is a deceiver and a betrayer. When Gloucester sides with the maltreated Lear, he is apprehended by Goneril and Regan, who blind him before turning him out of doors. The rejected Lear is also wandering outside, exposed to the elements and accompanied by the Fool (his jester). Eventually, the blind Gloucester and the deranged Lear meet, in a scene of great pathos.

By and by, the French army arrives in England to support Lear's cause, and before the decisive battle Lear and Cordelia are reconciled. But the French army is defeated by Goneril and Regan's forces, even though, by the intervention of Gloucester's loyal son, Edgar, the cruelty and perfidy of Goneril and Regan come to light, and both die (Goneril poisons Regan and then kills herself). Things seem then at last to be turning out favorably for Lear, but an order that had been given to execute Cordelia just fails to be countermanded, and at the end Lear comes on stage carrying her dead body. Shortly after, still holding her, Lear himself dies.

As Hazlitt reminds us, "all that we can say" about *King Lear* "must fall far short of the subject; or even of what we ourselves conceive of it",[35] and indeed no summary does justice to this complex, powerfully ragged yet majestically coherent play. Still, the foregoing remarks can at least make clear how the action focuses on Lear's fall from greatness, the perennial linchpin of tragedy, as Nuttall says. Lear's stature and habit of command are declared straight away in his display of royal power at the beginning of the play – even despite his erratic behavior – and then also in the fierce grandeur of his tempestuous, raging speeches of protest and anger on the heath where he is left to wander. As the play unfolds, Lear's fall from greatness is accompanied also by suffering so extreme, so disproportionate, and Cordelia's death is such a gratuitous cruelty, that we soon move beyond the simpler moral problem of Lear's egocentric arrogance as we find ourselves forced to consider what value we attach to the key scenes of forgiveness and reconciliation, given that everything of value for Lear is so senselessly destroyed. Even as he dies, Lear thinks that he sees Cordelia's lips move and that she is alive after all, and so he is denied even the dignity of the "recognition" that tragic heroes are often accorded in a flash of understanding that precedes their demise. By contrast, Lear's final words give voice only to the delusion that Cordelia is still alive, as language is emptied out, dislocated from the horror that he cannot, in the end, endure to face. And yet the play is packed with some of the most compelling poetry ever written, as Shakespeare brings home to us the weight of the problem of suffering, pitted against values that traditionally stand as a bulwark against despair and the loss of meaning. References throughout to the word "nature", for example, are especially resonant because of how they direct our attention to the core problem of assessing the nature of human nature. The word also inheres in a pattern of further, analogous motifs, so that a richly organized language runs by way of a great many aquifers, often turbulent, bewilderingly indirect, yet feeding together the deep, still waters into which we are finally led. Throughout *King Lear,* different senses of "nature" force us repeatedly to assess whether or not humans are governed mainly by selfishness and animal appetite, in contrast to the values that transcend these impulses and in so doing indicate what is properly human about us. According to the hard, let us say Hobbesian view, Lear says to the raving and naked beggar Poor Tom that "the thing itself" is "no more but such a poor, bare, forked animal as thou art" (III, 4, 106–107). Yet elsewhere, the Gentleman explains to Lear, "Thou hast one daughter /Who redeems Nature" (IV, 6, 206), pointing us (anachronistically, we might notice) toward the Christian idea that the effects on nature of the Fall caused by the transgression of Adam and Eve can be reversed by self-giving love, as Cordelia (like Jesus) "redeems Nature from the general curse /Which twain have brought her to" (IV, 6, 206). As is touchingly evident in the scenes of reconciliation (and even in the villain Edmund's willingness to "exchange charity" [V, 3, 168] as he is dying), we might feel that human beings are not in all respects reducible to their self-seeking instincts and animal appetites. After all, do not humans create culture in excess of their basic material needs and without which they are not fully themselves? One of Lear's most memorable speeches addresses this point directly. As Goneril and Regan go about ruthlessly depriving him of his retinue on the grounds that he does not "need" all those people around him, he protests with a mixture of grief and indignation:

> O reason not the need! Our basest beggars
> Are in the poorest thing superfluous.
> Allow not nature more than nature needs,
> Man's life is cheap as beast's (II, 4, 261–264)

Here Lear points out that the human is constituted by a surplus ("more than nature") beyond the mere sufficiency of the "beast's" animal existence. As he goes on to say, his daughters' "gorgeous" clothes are in themselves evidence of this excess of culture over nature, but in denying the same to him, they become "unnatural hags" (II, 4, 275) not knowing what the nature of human nature is. Earlier, Goneril and Regan had seen Lear's old age as mere "dotage" (II, 4, 194), and advised him, "being weak, seem so" (II, 4, 198). In their eyes, age is a biological condition equivalent to physical vulnerability. By contrast, Lear describes himself as "a poor old man /As full of grief as age" as he struggles for "patience" (II, 4, 268–270). This is closer to the Duke of Albany's view of Lear as "a father, and a gracious agèd man" (IV, 2, 42), a statement in keeping with the traditional "policy and reverence of age" (I, 2, 47) that Gloucester reads about in a letter planted by his villainous son Edmund, who is attempting to subvert those same humane values. Although Goneril and Regan allude frequently to Lear's age, for them he is merely an "idle old man" and, as they insist, "old fools are babes again" (I, 3, 16–19). Traditional, culturally validated respect for age and station does not feature in their naturalistic reckoning. Lear's speech of protest and dis-illusion is a preface to his wanderings on the heath, where he curses the world's injustice with such violence that the stormy weather seems barely adequate to mirror the tempestuous force of his language. As we see, in the earlier speech he struggles for "patience" and barely holds back tears ("Let not women's weapons, water drops, /Stain my man's cheeks" [II, 4, 274–275]). But his vulnerability then swerves into a compensatory, electrifying anger: "No, you unnatural hags! /I will have such revenges on you both" (II, 4, 275–276). He only gradually realizes that this con-flict within himself between a humiliating awareness of his weakness and an overpowering, vindictive rage is beginning to threaten his wits: "O Fool, I shall go mad!" (II, 4, 283), he says, and the stage direction in-dicates "storm and tempest". It is as if the contest between nature and culture takes place within him, as his personal appeal on behalf of human dignity clashes with the autocratic impersonality of the cosmic curses he calls down. Also, as the old king rages wildly, grandly, on the heath, the Fool provides a commentary, bringing the cosmic protests and imprecations back down to practical matters: "Good nuncle, in; ask thy daughters blessing. Here's a night pities neither wise men nor fools" (III, 2, 11–13). By calling attention to Lear's actual, material predica-ment, the Fool confirms that the old king's mighty rhetoric is as delusional as it is impressive as he summons nature to his defense:

> Blow, winds, and crack your cheeks. Rage, blow!
> You cataracts and hurricanoes, spout
> Till you have drenched our steeples, drowned the cocks.
> You sulph'rous and thought-executing fires,

Vaunt-couriers of oak-cleaving thunderbolts,
Singe my white head. And thou, all-shaking thunder,
Strike flat the thick rotundity o' th' world,
Crack Nature's molds, all germains spill at once,
That makes ingrateful man. (III, 2, 1–9)

The immense presumption of calling down the elemental forces of nature to execute a wholesale apocalyptic revenge gathers here an almost hierophantic momentum. But then, in a moment of crazed pathos, Lear stalls in order to exempt the elements from reproof – "I tax not you, you elements, with unkindness" (III, 2, 16) – faltering into the realization that he is, in fact "a poor, infirm, weak, and despised old man" (III, 2, 20). The extraordinary power of Lear's great speeches on the heath is that, despite his vulnerability and grief, his Olympian arrogance remains defiantly persistent, even when shot through with moments of bewildered pathos, or crossed with self-pity and dawning insight that he nonetheless is unable really to accept. "He hath ever but slenderly known himself" (I, 1, 293) says Goneril, coldly correct, and as Lear's mind falters, his language also teeters on the edge of incoherence, torn by its own inner tensions and contradictions.

There is a great deal of crazy talk in *King Lear*, whether from Poor Tom (Edgar disguised as a mad beggar) or in the Fool's riddles and jibes (he could well be a "natural" fool, which is to say, mentally challenged) or in Lear's ravings. Much that is spoken stands on the very edge of dissolution, or delusion, or madness, and in reaching toward the tragic catharsis, the dialogue seems gradually to turn against itself, under such pressure that its own frame of reference splits from within. Yet one of the most telling ways in which the efficacy of speech is canceled – or brought to the very brink of silence – is not by an overload of wild language, but by an insistent echoing throughout the play of a single word, a single negation, often spoken sotto voce but with a power that reduces all of Lear's grand gestures to, well, nothing.[36]

"Nothing, my lord" (I, 1, 87) is Cordelia's minimalist reply to Lear's crass request for praise in the opening scene. Perhaps she is too stubborn – too much her father's daughter – as she refuses to play along and then digs in. He, incredulous, replies, "Nothing?". "Nothing", she repeats. "Nothing will come of nothing" (I, 1, 87–90), says Lear, rising to anger and hinting that she will get no inheritance if she keeps on like that. But she does not relent, and he repays her silence by disinheriting her, which is to say, giving her nothing.

The word "nothing" is picked up also in the subplot, when Gloucester asks what letter Edmund is reading, and Edmund, now that he sees Gloucester falling into his trap, says, mock-guiltily, "Nothing, my lord" – echoing Cordelia's very words. Gloucester replies that "the quality of nothing hath not such need to hide itself" (I, 2, 31), and he snatches the letter, which, of course, gives him wrong information. Here again, an inheritance is in the balance, as Edmund seeks to oust his brother.

Throughout the play, the word "nothing" retains its strong connection to quantification, but we are also asked to consider the worth of human values that cannot be quantified and which are, as it were, also nothing, in the sense that they cannot be counted like an inheritance. Thus, when the Fool recites a riddling speech to Lear, concluding with the lines, "and thou shalt have more /Than two tens to a score" (I, 4, 128–129), Lear replies, "This is nothing, Fool", and the Fool asks, "Can you make no use of nothing, nuncle?" (I, 4, 130 ff). The Fool's numbers don't make sense because, taken literally, two tens *are* a score. By contrast, the "more" to which the Fool directs Lear's attention is the "nothing" for which Lear has no use, as spoken by Cordelia who so resolutely refused to quantify her love for her father. Later, during the reconciliation scene with Cordelia, Lear suggests that she has good reason, or "cause", to be offended, and she replies, "No cause, no cause" (IV, 7, 75). Here Shakespeare offers a variation on the idea of the incalculable nothing, the love that Cordelia offered Lear and which cost her inheritance. And so, by declaring "nothing", language itself stands on the brink of silence, which is, for the reconciled Lear and Cordelia, also the silence of communion – even though the other silence, the silence of abjection, has not yet fully had its say. But then Cordelia dies, and Lear's hammer-blow repetition – "Never, never, never, never, never" (V, 3, 310) – gives us, through the cadence of the mighty pentameter, a final recitation of a victorious negation, a last word declaring the scandal of grief, suffering, and loss against which all the consoling antidotes break to pieces. In a telling moment, in the last lines of the play Edgar instructs the assembled company – as well as the audience, surely – to "speak what we feel, not what we ought to say" (V, 3, 326). It is almost as if Shakespeare was uneasy about the power of what he had released, but it seems clear that Edgar does not want us running for cover from the terrifying vision, in search of some clichéd consolation.

Dialogue and "the time that is left"

Painful though *King Lear* is, I want nonetheless to stop short of claiming that it pitches us utterly into hopelessness. There is a difference, after all, between King Lear the man and *King Lear* the play, and Karl Jaspers[37] focuses on this distinction between protagonist and spectator to point out that although tragedy attempts to express a terrible, finally inexpressible truth about the human condition, it does so by means of language that gives the spectator access to the protagonist's experience. That is, the formal means of expression puts us at a distance from the dreadful truths that are brought home to us, and we remain sufficiently (if not entirely) insulated, able to contemplate the hard facts that are emotionally draining but not so destructive that we cannot think about what they might mean for us. And so Schopenhauer's "terrifying side of life" touches us but does not consume us, as reflection brings us to understand – not just in the conceptual domain but also in an imaginative thinking infused by emotion – that indeed there is no safe haven, no sufficient justice, no adequate solace, no convincing answer to the problem of suffering. The pleromatic silence of the saints and the desolate silence of the abject victims are therefore not the only kinds of silence to engage us. There is also a silence of contemplation, or reflection, which is where tragedy brings us and which is a consequence, a product, even, of the dialogical, both within the immense complexities of a play such as *King Lear* and through our interaction with it.

As we see, throughout *King Lear* the dialogue comprises an extraordinary polyphonic variety of voices, ranging from the pre-articulate realm of primal feeling to the gestural and mimetic, mythic and narrative, as well as the conceptually sophisticated. To adapt the blind Gloucester's words to Lear, we see the play feelingly, as the art of the drama forces us also to the very limits of language in order to produce a felt understanding of the tragic dimension of life that is capable, in turn, of effecting a transformation in ourselves and in our relationships with others. In *Tragedy Is Not Enough*, Karl Jaspers interprets tragedy as a step toward a fuller understanding that contains the hard truths about injustice and guiltless suffering that it depicts. But also for Jaspers, as an aristocratic genre, tragedy does not engage sufficiently with people's ordinary concerns, and so we need to relocate the tragic vision within "a larger context of fundamental reality",[38] which is to say, within the common life.

Jaspers is helpfully supplemented here by Gadamer's observation that tragedy brings about a "pensiveness" that is indeed "a kind of affirmation, return to ourselves". That is, the "disproportionate, terrible immensity" of the suffering that tragedy depicts makes a claim on the spectator, which should lead then to "a genuine communion" with other people based on a deeper, shared knowledge of the world.[39] It is as if we understand that "the worst" is always a terrifying potential of our own lives, even though the worst has not yet occurred, because we can still talk to each other. We still have time, that is, whereas the tragic hero does not. Edith Wyschogrod writes about "death and the time that is left", pointing out that in his account of death, Heidegger omits the fact that "the force of the relation to my own death derives from an awareness of *the time that is left*, the gap between my life now and the event that is my dying and is yet to come".[40] As far as tragedy is concerned, the death of the hero brings home in a strong form the scandal of death itself, but then throws us back, pensively, on the fact that we have time left. In turn, this realization is infused with the understanding (however tacit) that death gives meaning to our remaining time. Also, because the worst is not yet, the time remaining is the time of dialogue, which cannot remain innocent of tragedy, because in marking the limitations of dialogue, tragedy shapes the spirit in which dialogue is conducted.

Still, we might also feel that there is something not quite sufficient in Gadamer's idea alone of reflective contemplation and tragic "pensiveness", for does this not seem an inducement, as it were, to passivity? And so I want to end by returning to the note of defiance in the Nietzschean conviction that there is something "indestructibly joyful and powerful"[41] about life, calling for affirmation despite the worst that the world might do. Albert Camus, in the wake of both Dostoyevsky and Nietzsche, likewise saw unflinchingly into the heart of the absurdity, the blind suffering of the human condition, in the face of which he chose to celebrate the simple immediacy of the Mediterranean sunlight and through it the life force itself.[42] The point is not to deny the truths that tragedy reveals but, as Hegel recommends, to look the negative in the face in order to negate the negation, because the Spirit cannot otherwise express itself.

Van Gogh: "sorrowful, yet always rejoicing"

Vincent van Gogh brings together these concluding points about defiance and affirmation in an especially compelling way because of the remarkable symbiosis between his paintings and his letters. The paintings of course are famous, endlessly reproduced, often cheaply commercialized, frequently parodied. An iris or a sunflower might as readily turn up on a shower curtain in Tokyo, a shopping bag in London, or a beer mat in Brussels. There is even a packet of potato chips called "The Potato Eaters" for sale in the Van Gogh Museum in Amsterdam. But visit that museum any day, time, or season and you find it also full of people – visitors of every age, nationality, and condition, thronging in a perpetual vigil. They are drawn not only by the paintings but by the man, whose difficult and, in the end, tragic life is so bound up with his art that homage to the man and admiration of his paintings have become all but inseparable. In a recent article, the film critic Anthony Lane[43] wonders about the unusually persistent interest of filmmakers in van Gogh's life, and one main reason is surely that van Gogh's biography is so gripping and so fused with the confrontational, urgent force of the paintings that his personal narrative provides a privileged access also to his art. It is especially significant that this personal narrative is so largely supplied by van Gogh's own hand, and 3,800-some pages of his letters are rightly praised as a literary achievement of the highest order. Reading all the way through leaves you feeling as you might after reading a series of Dostoyevsky novels back to back. Certainly, van Gogh's extraordinary writerly talents were not lost on his sister-in-law, Jo van Gogh-Bonger, who inherited the large collection of Vincent's paintings that were in her husband Theo's possession when he died some six months after his brother. As it happens, Theo also held the bulk of Vincent's surviving letters (658 from a total of 819), and Jo saw immediately that the bonds between these two bodies of work would be fundamental to what became her lifelong mission – namely, the promotion of van Gogh the painter. The story of this undertaking was not fully told until recently in the brilliant biography of Jo by Hans Luijten,[44] who for the first time has had access to the relevant family documents. But one thing that has been clear from the start is that Jo used the letters to promote Vincent's art, and still today in the Van Gogh Museum the large-print banners strategically placed between the paintings to provide information to viewers draw heavily on Vincent's own words.

Broadly, the letters attest to the intensity of van Gogh's commitment and the integrity of his vision. They describe the physical and mental anguish that caused him to be hospitalized and the fierce affirmation of life from the heart of disappointment and tragedy. Also, they tell us a great deal about painting, and how in his own practice, Vincent sought to achieve expressive power by deliberate exaggeration and by insisting on the beauty of unconventional subjects – poor people, peasants, miners, prostitutes, laborers, the world-weary. We learn also about his favorite idea that deliberately incorporated imperfections, "inaccuracies", can produce an effect "truer than the literal truth" (515)[45] because the imperfection of the truly beautiful awakens longing for an elusive completeness, and with that longing a deep nostalgia.

And so the letters tell a powerful story, but more relevant to the present chapter is the fact that they also have all the lineaments of tragedy, showing us a fearfully disproportionate suffering brought down upon a gifted protagonist through an all too probable and yet fatal combination of character and circumstance, leaving us emotionally worn out, as tragedy does, and wondering about the injustice of it all.

Interestingly, from early in the letters, van Gogh repeatedly cites St. Paul's injunction to be "sorrowful, yet always rejoicing" (2 Corinthians 6:10). After he gives up his allegiance to orthodox Christianity, the references to scripture – including this one – drop almost completely out of his correspondence. But the spirit of the once-favored Pauline verse persists in his resolve to defy sorrow not by avoiding it but by pushing through to a further, encompassing affirmation. And so in his paintings he strove especially "to say something consoling" in the teeth of human deprivation, and to this end he wanted "to paint men or women with that *je ne sais quoi* of the eternal, of which the halo used to be the symbol" (673). The paintings stand, then, as a powerful response to the tragic vision that the letters present, and the rough, immediate vigor, the surging colors that are at once a confrontation and an embrace, the fierce celebration of the natural miracle of existence, are as powerfully captivating as they are distinctive. Still, this is not to say that the paintings are untouched by the tragic dimension or that the letters are joyless. There is deep grief on the edge of nightmare, for example, in the paintings of the Saint-Rémy hospital, and even the glorious sunflowers are past their prime, touched already by the withering hand of time. Nonetheless, the letters tell a tragic story to which the sunflowers are van Gogh's best answer, and it is worth noticing as well that the sunflowers return us to the ordinary. In van Gogh's time they were a common plant, used for fodder and not considered valuable. There is nothing refined – nothing "aristocratic" – in their appeal, and in this they are equivalent, perhaps, to Camus's turning to the everyday experience of the Mediterranean sunshine, and to Jaspers's bringing us back to a transfigured ordinariness at the far side of the tragic catharsis. As we see, Nietzsche insists that we need Apollo even though he is a dreamer who lives in a world of illusion – a common world that we think of as ordinary, rational, ordered. Also, we need the illusion of desire, which Lacan insists we do not give up even though it cannot be fulfilled and binds us inextricably with the "death which the lack at the heart of desire prefigures".[46] Death, after all, makes one's life real, and we live authentically only by embracing our own finitude. During "the time that is left", as Edith Wyschogrod says, the worst is not yet because we can still talk about it, as Edgar insists. And we can best go on talking about it in the place of dialogue, between the silences of fullness and abjection. We do not do well if we lose sight of either of these limit conditions, and this is so because dialogue without a tragic vision is frivolous, just as dialogue without desire is sterile. Theodicy and its imagined consolations do indeed break against the problem of evil, but it is best nonetheless to be on the side of whatever life-affirming protest can be managed in the circumstances – to be on the side of the sunflowers.

Notes

1 See Caroline Walker Bynum, "Material Continuity, Personal Survival, and the Resurrection of the Body: A Scholastic Discussion in its Medieval and Modern Contexts", *History of Religions* 30 (1), 1990, 51–85.
2 See, for example, *Abyakatasmyutta*, "The Book of the Six Sense Bases", *The Connected Discourses of the Buddha. A Translation of the Samyutta Nikaya*, trans. Bikkhu Bodhi (Boston: Wisdom Publications, 2000), p. 1394.
3 *Tao Te Ching*, 13.
4 Dmitri Nikulin, *Dialectic and Dialogue* (Stanford: Stanford University Press, 2010), p. x.
5 Robert N. Bellah, *Religion in Human Evolution*, pp. 350 ff.
6 Friedrich Nietzsche, *The Birth of Tragedy*, in *The Birth of Tragedy and the Genealogy of Morals*, trans. Francis Golffing (New York: Doubleday, 1956), p. 57.
7 St. Teresa of Avila, *The Life of St. Teresa of Jesus*, trans. David Lewis (London: Thomas Baker, 1916), chapter XVIII, 2.
8 Lao Tzu, *Tao Te Ching*, trans. Gia-Fu Feng and Jane English, with an Introduction by Jacob Needleman (New York: Vintage, 1989; translation first published, 1972), p. 3.
9 *The Diamond Sūtra*, 7. See *The Diamond Sūtra and the Sūtra of Hui-Neng*, trans. A.F. Price and Wong Mou-Lam (Boston: Shambhala, 1990), p. 24.
10 *St. Bernard's Sermons on the Canticle of Canticles*, translated by a priest of Mount Mellary, 2 vols. (Dublin: Browne and Nolan, 1920), Sermon LXXI; *The Complete Works of Saint John of the Cross*, trans. and edited by E. Allison Peers, three volumes in one (Hertfordshire: Anthony Clarke, 1974), III, 162.
11 AE (George William Russell), *The Candle of Vision. The Autobiography of a Mystic* (Illinois: Theosophical Publishing House, 1974), p. 20.
12 William of St. Thierry, *The Enigma of Faith*, 3. See *The Enigma of Faith*, trans. John D. Anderson (Washington, D.C.: Cistercian Publications, 1974), p. 37.
13 Simone Weil, "The *Iliad* or the Poem of Force", in *Simone Weil. An Anthology,* ed. and introduced by Siân Miles (London: Virago, 1986), p. 204.

14 Richard Davis, *Mirror Hate. The Convergent Ideology of Northern Ireland Paramilitaries, 1966–1992* (Aldershot: Darmouth, 1994), p. 3, *et passim*.

15 John Hewitt, "The Iron Circle", *The Collected Poems of John Hewitt*, ed. Frank Ormsby (Belfast: Blackstaff, 1991), p. 142.

16 Patrick Bishop and Eamonn Mallie, *The Provisional IRA* (London: Corgi, 1997; first published, 1987), p. 195, citing a source using the pseudonym "McShane".

17 Eamon Collins (with Mick McGovern), *Killing Rage* (London: Granta, 1998; first published, 1997), p. 2.

18 Michael Asher, *Shoot to Kill: A Soldier's Journey Through Violence* (London: Penguin, 1990), p. 120.

19 Karl Jaspers, *The Origin and Goal of History* (New Haven: Yale University Press, 1953), p. 127. See Richard Madsen, "The Future of Transcendence. A Sociological Agenda", in *The Axial Age and its Consequences*, ed. Robert N. Bellah and Hans Joas (Cambridge, Mass: Harvard University Press, 2012), p. 431.

20 Martin Buber, *I and Thou*, trans. Ronald Gregor Smith (New York: Charles Scribner's Sons, 1958), p. 5: "O accumulation of information! It, always it!". See also, p. 48: "The communal life of man can no more than man himself dispense with the world of *It*".

21 William Law, *The Spirit of Prayer*, in *The Spirit of Prayer and the Spirit of Love,* ed. Sidney Spencer (Cambridge: James Clarke, 1969), p. 138. See Patrick Grant, *Spiritual Discourse and the Meaning of Persons* (London: Macmillan, 1994), chapter 6, "Imagination and the Transfiguring of Nature", pp. 114–133, and especially pp. 124 ff.

22 On the transfiguration as a misplaced resurrection story, see Patrick Grant, *Spiritual Discourse and the Meaning of Persons*, pp. 24 ff, and p. 183, note 10.

23 Ovid, *Tristia ex Ponto* (Cambridge, Mass.: Harvard University Press, 1996), p. 83; John Milton, Preface to *Samson Agonistes*, "Of that Sort of Dramatic Poem which is call'd Tragedy", in John Milton. *Collected Poems and Major Prose*, ed. Merritt Y. Hughes (New York: Odyssey, 1957), p. 549; Arthur Schopenhauer, *The World as Will and Idea*, trans. R.B. Haldane and J. Kemp (London: Kegan Paul, Trench, Trubner, 1907), p. 326.

24 The following summaries are based on Aristotle, *Poetics*, trans. Gerald F. Else (Ann Arbor: University of Michigan Press, 1970).

25 Terry Eagleton, *The Event of Literature* (New Haven: Yale University Press, 2012), pp. 19 ff.

26 A.D. Nuttall, *Why Does Tragedy Give Pleasure?* (Oxford: Clarendon Press, 1996), p. 82. Further page numbers are cited in the text.

27 "The delight of tragedy proceeds from our consciousness of fiction". See Samuel Johnson, "Preface to Shakespeare", in *Johnson on Shakespeare*, ed. Artur Sherbo, vol. vii of the Yale edition of the Works of Samuel Johnson, 15 vols. (New Haven: Yale University Press, 1958–85), vol. vii, p. 78.

28 See my remarks on Gadamer in Chapter 3. Jean Grondin, *The Philosophy of Gadamer*, trans. Kathryn Plant (Montreal and Kingston: McGill-Queen's University Press, 2003; first published, 1999), p. 36, states the point well: "If the work of art allows us to escape from ordinary life, it is only to drag us back all the more, so that we rediscover our reality,

unveiled by art, with new eyes and ears. Far from erasing it, art always presupposes our continuous existence". See Wolfgang Iser, *The Act of Reading: A Theory of Aesthetic Response* (Baltimore: The Johns Hopkins University Press, 1978), pp. 69 ff.

29 "I was so many years ago so shocked by Cordelia's death, that I know not whether I ever endured to read again the last scenes of the play till I undertook to revise them as an editor". See, *Johnson on Shakespeare*, vol. viii, p. 704.

30 I refer here again to Bellah. See above, note 5.

31 *The Birth of Tragedy and The Genealogy of Morals*, p. 126.

32 *The World as Will and Idea*, p. 327.

33 See W.B. Yeats, "The Gyres": "We that look on but laugh in tragic joy".

34 The following references are to *King Lear*, ed. Russell Baker, *The Complete Signet Shakespeare*, ed. Sylvan Barnet (New York: Harcourt Brace Jovanovich, 1972). References are cited in the text.

35 William Hazlitt, *Characters of Shakespeare's Plays* (London: Oxford University Press, 1955; first published, 1817), p. 119.

36 The density and complexity of the patterned language of the play are dealt with often by commentators, and with special thoroughness in the early study by Robert Heilman, on whom I draw broadly in the following account. See Robert Bechtold Heilman, *This Great Stage: Image and Structure in "King Lear"* (Baton Rouge: Louisiana State University Press, 1948).

37 See Karl Jaspers, *Tragedy Is Not Enough*, trans. Harold A.T. Reiche, Harry T Moore, and Karl W. Deutsch (Boston: Beacon Press, 1952; first published, 1947).

38 *Tragedy Is Not Enough*, p. 80.

39 Hans Georg Gadamer, *Truth and Method*, translation revised by Joel Weinsheimer and Donald G. Marshall (London: Bloomsbury, 2013), pp. 132–3.

40 Edith Wyschogrod, *Saints and Postmodernism. Revisioning Moral Philosophy* (Chicago: University of Chicago Press, 1990), p. 64.

41 *The Birth of Tragedy*, p. 50.

42 Albert Camus, "The New Mediterranean Culture" (1937), available online, *Hellenic Antidote*, Wednesday, 8 March, 2017. See also Neil Foxlee, *"The New Mediterranean Culture": A Text and its Contexts*, Modern French Studies 38 (Oxford: Peter Lang, 2010).

43 Anthony Lane, "Why Do Filmmakers Love Van Gogh?" *The New Yorker*, November 19, 2018.

44 Hans Luijten, *Alles voor Vincent. Het Leven van Jo van Gogh-Bonger* (Amsterdam: Prometheus, 2019). An English translation is planned for 2020.

45 *Vincent van Gogh—The Letters*, ed. Leo Jansen, Hans Luijten, and Nienke Bakker, 6 vols. (New York: Thames and Hudson, 2009). Letter numbers are cited in the text.

46 Terry Eagleton, *Sweet Violence. The Idea of the Tragic* (Oxford: Blackwell, 2003), p. 233, commenting on Lacan's injunction, "Do not give up on your desire!".

5   Aporia and epiphany

Bearings in the bricolage

The protean energy of language that Bakhtin describes as heteroglossia is infused, we now see, with the similarly unquenchable
proliferations of desire. The longing for reconciliation, meaning, liberation from the past, and an experience of union in which desire is
brought to rest is part of what constitutes us as a species who can
generate complex meanings linguistically and use imagination to
ponder the perennial gulf between what is and what might (or ought
to) be. As we have seen in Chapter 3, Jacques Lacan did not share
Augustine's belief that the gulf between desire and fulfillment can
be closed at last in the vision of God. But Lacan saw that Augustine
understood the economy and dynamics of desire very well and knew
with what alacrity we deflect longing into whatever substitute objects
we imagine will provide lasting gratification, even though in fact they
never do. Such a general understanding of the incessant reduplication
of desire is often enough restated through the centuries, and so it seems
that within the walls of the world as we know it there is no closure,
no final convergence of love and understanding, desire and language –
a fact which, in turn, helps to explain why so many people keep
looking expectantly to an afterlife.

Meanwhile, in the here and now the tangles of heteroglossia go on
being reproduced in the corporeal and historical labyrinths out of
which language emerges in search of the desired but unattainable
fullness of meaning. Through language we discover also the contrast
between the ideal and the actual, and in that context the problem of
pain and the scandal of suffering. A tragic view of the human predicament might enable us then within the everyday world perhaps
to be less confident about being in control, more compassionate, more
inclined to proceed with a frisson perhaps of fear and trembling in

light of an enhanced sense of contingency, more prepared for reversals of fortune and the arbitrary unfairness of life.

In light of all this, I have argued that dialogue is the mode of discourse best fitted to enable us to engage fruitfully with others, given that we are never without contradictions, asymmetries, and unsatisfied aspirations, so that for individual people, as in society in general, different aspects of language remain perpetually in conflict. Many traditional cultures take their bearings still today from ancient rituals and the mythological narratives recorded in sacred books, and as a result are often ill at ease with the conceptual and critical tools developed in the Axial Age and subsequently informing modern scientific enquiry and the emergence of secularism. As Donald writes, the mythical and theoretical "collide daily in a globalised economy",[1] and one main, pressing challenge of the modern world is to mediate the all but endless variety of conflicts arising from these collisions. In turn, the collisions themselves are not simply between the religious-mythical and secular-theoretical. There is a vast, further cross-fertilization and mutual criticism between and within the traditions themselves, which go on producing fissures and refractions as well as new syntheses and consolidations. As Charles Taylor points out, "it is a pluralist world, in which many forms of belief and unbelief jostle and hence fragilize each other", and in the ensuing "bricolage"[2] of interpretations and styles of allegiance, the monolithic truth claims of no single religious tradition can today credibly be accorded absolute pre-eminence. Meanwhile, secularism itself, through its close ties to the global capitalist enterprise, has seen its critical force increasingly squandered in subservience to the rituals of consumerism, the cult of celebrity, and the sacralizing of the individual. Nonetheless, the hard-won right to unbelief remains a major achievement of secularism that continues to protect against the excesses of organized religion. Yet the freedom of critical enquiry and the pluralism that secularism promotes have also contributed greatly to a fragmentation of discourse and a relativizing of traditional values to the point of such radical uncertainty that control passes all the more easily to those whose interests are merely pragmatic and expedient.

Addressing this broad state of affairs, Edith Wyschogrod looks to a renovated postmodernism to provide, out of this very fragmentation and relativity, some new assessment of personal values based on a "recognition of the primacy of the other person and the dissolution of self-interest".[3] Such an assessment is a necessary condition also of dialogue as I have been describing it, and which likewise has to meet the challenges of the postmodern bricolage, intensified now especially by social media and digital communication. As I pointed out in Chapter 2, in these new, fast-developing arenas of discourse the interlocutor is, simply, not fully enough there. The impact of the expressive body, the personal immediacy that elicits respect, the complex and often tacit responsiveness geared to the interplay of narratives and concepts that in turn follow the rhythm of an exchange – all this is largely absent from the efficient minimalism of the Facebook and Twitter messages that so readily privilege the gratifications of negation and denunciation. By contrast, decorum, thoughtfulness, expertise, patient consideration, and an ability to listen that transcends self-interest are given short shrift. And yet, through the bricolage, dialogue also seeks its opportunity.

This book is by no means exempt from the challenges and difficulties I have just set out. Indeed, as a response to the looming catastrophe of climate change, the threat of nuclear proliferation, mass migrations of refugees and asylum-seekers, reckless trade wars, the widening gap between the ultrarich and everyone else, the suggestion that it would be a good thing to practice dialogue is a straw in the wind. And yet a failure of nerve offers even less, and it is well to remember that through the broad range of human arts and sciences and along the immense spectrum of human learning and expertise, dialogue is in fact already a medium for creative thinking and new understanding. Moreover, countless people in many walks of life are well aware both of the overarching problems and of what Charles Taylor calls a "diffuse" and "widespread"[4] sense of some large change in the making, even if there is as yet no common language sufficient to consolidate the will for productive and radical reform. Yet without dialogue there will be no shaping force, no way ahead, and this is so because the prevailing dissonance will not become harmonious by constraint, but through the personalist presuppositions and the processes of learning that dialogue embodies, as I have attempted to show. Meanwhile, the dead ends, confusions, and contradictions remain with us. They are what is meant by aporia, which is to say "without passage" (*a-poria*), impassible, stuck, confused, at a loss.

Inhabiting aporia

The sense of not knowing the way ahead, of being at a loss, is a central theme already in the tales of the *Odyssey* and the biblical narratives of the Jahwist compiler. But in Homer and the Bible the main journeys have a direction toward a homecoming, a promised land that is a shared goal, a communal gratification. By contrast, in the current cultural phase the sense of traveling together is largely replaced by being frantically at work, dancing furiously on the spot with no direction beyond exigent accumulation, often in order merely to secure one's basic needs. A small number of fortunate aspirants are allowed the gratifications of wealth, the trappings of glamour, the self-satisfactions of benevolence, and indulgence in the embellishments of so-called "culture". What is more pleasing, after all, than to be validated by the admiring and envious gaze of others who want the same imagined "success" by way of a self-aggrandizement that in fact pre-empts any real fulfillment and the chance of any homecoming at all?

This is not to say that the biblical journey to the promised land and the Homeric *nostos* are without setbacks, dead ends, confusions. Part of Plato's grand project was to recast Homer in a philosophical mode with Socrates replacing the epic hero, and Plato depicts dialogue also as a journey fraught with setbacks and aporias, as the participants often experience disorientation, not knowing where the discussion might turn and finding themselves at a loss for words. Still, as Plato insists, in dialogue not knowing what to think next or how to proceed can also be a creative part of the process. The point is that there is a process, which in turn is a declaration of resistance to according finality to the aporia. As with tragedy, here again we soon find ourselves pressing up against the scandal of suffering and the enigma of death, the last, unavoidable "no way out" in the face of which we stand confounded. Plato was well aware of the problem, not only because of the tragic death of his heroic Socrates but also by way of the eschatological myths that he invented to address the question of whether or not aporia does have the last word after all.

It is helpful at this point to turn to Jacques Derrida,[5] who, with characteristic, scrupulous attention to the limits of discourse, considers precisely this topic – the relationship between aporia and death. On the one hand, Derrida observes that my own death is intimately mine and I go through it alone. On the other hand, my death cannot be said to be mine because "I" am no longer the subject of the experience, which is why I am said to be dead. That is, we never have the experience of our own demise, and as far as crossing "the ultimate border" is concerned, "who has ever done it and who can testify to it?" The aporia therefore declares itself as "the difficult or the impracticable, here the impossible, passage, the refused, denied, or prohibited passage, indeed the nonpassage" (8). But is it possible to have any experience at all of this non-passage, given that there would be no bearings, no markers or boundaries to enable an identification of the aporia which ceases to be "*as such*" (33) when it is given a name, a place, a local habitation? In light of these considerations, Derrida concludes that the "ultimate aporia" is not death but "the impossibility of the aporia *as such*" (78). With reference to Heidegger, he goes on to argue that Dasein's[6] relation to death "is not dissociable from its ability to speak" (74), because the capacity for language enables Dasein to question its own existence and to choose resolutely in an angst-ridden awareness of the inevitable temporal limitation, which is to say death. And so, however tacitly, death gives life direction and meaning. Derrida also describes how in an earlier study he "suggested that a sort of nonpassive endurance of the aporia was the condition of responsibility and of decision" (16). And so, as with death, the aporia "*as such*" does not appear but presents itself as an impasse that has already inscribed within it the disposition toward finding a way, while there is time, through an unexpected opening (*poros*) that brings to light some new manner of seeing and understanding that in turn can engender a fresh sense of responsibility and decision.

Derrida's "nonpassive endurance of the aporia" is also central to what I take dialogue to be, insofar as, through dialogue, people encounter challenges without seeing where a solution lies, but are sustained nonetheless by a shared commitment to the emergence of some more adequate understanding, some new possibilities for creative choice, however inchoate. As I have suggested throughout this book, such a process is not impersonal or conducted solely at the conceptual level. Rather, it folds back upon the narrative and poetic dimensions of language, and is dramatic (that is, mimetic) insofar as it addresses crises and transformations in how people think and feel and relate to one another. As particular aporias are encountered and lived through, the aporetic then itself is reconfigured in ever-new questions, doubts, challenges. Plato's early, so-called "aporetic" dialogues (such as the *Meno* and *Protagoras*) are deliberately unresolved in order to produce a sort of fertile perplexity, but this effect is not entirely absent in the grander, apparently more resolved conclusions of dialogues such as the *Republic* and *Timaeus*. There we are left with philosophical speculation shaped into the complex open-endedness of poetry and myth that in turn give rise to new dissatisfactions as we are brought up against the limits of what we know for sure.

Here we might be reminded yet again that Plato was the great originator of dialogue as a literary form, in which the process of oral communication is presented in a manner that we assess through reading. Not surprisingly, numerous aporias are encountered in this process, but the participants within the dialogue as well as the

readers are sustained by an expectation that their mutual engagement can discover a way out, a *poros*, a fresh way of looking that
intimates something yet further to be understood, some continuing
transfiguration of the habitual.

Nicholas Rescher's well-argued book *Aporetics: Rational Deliberation
in the Face of Inconsistency*, considers difficulties that arise when people
realize that their thinking comprises "individually plausible but collectively incompatible theses",[7] and his analysis demonstrates the value of
clear thinking and careful discrimination in dealing with many conceptual inconsistencies with which we routinely live, often without noticing them. Socrates also was much concerned with these problems, but
an account of aporia in Plato's dialogues as a whole requires us also to
consider the substrate of metaphor, myth, and mimesis underpinning
the conceptual meaning of the aporetic on which Rescher concentrates.
As I have emphasized throughout, dialogue cannot dispense with any of
the layers that mark the main breakthroughs in the evolution of language without diminishing, or sidelining, some significant aspect of how
we relate to one another. With this in mind, let us now turn to some
mythic and poetic aspects of aporia.

Travels with Plato: sailors and cave-dwellers

Sarah Kofman's remarkable work on the idea of aporia in ancient
Greek philosophy[8] focuses, as she says, on "the semantic richness of
poros and *aporia*" to show how these words belong within a "family"
(9) of metaphors and stories that constitute a tradition. Within this
tradition, *poros* means a path or way out, but also carries a suggestion
of expediency, of something achieved through ingenuity. This further
suggestion is explained by the fact that, as a mythological figure, Porus
is the son of Metis, inventor of stratagems, expedients, and ingenious
devisings. Strategic planning and resourcefulness are therefore part
of Porus's makeup as son of Metis. Also, as Kofman says, *poros* needs
to be distinguished from *odos*. Both words mean a path or road, but
"*poros* refers only to a sea-route or a route down a river, to a passage
opened up across a chaotic expanse". It follows that "a *poros* is never
traced in advance, that it can always be obliterated, that it must always
be traced anew" (10). Although landmarks and "points of light" can
help with plotting a course, the sea itself remains untracked and preserves no traces; rather, it is an "endless realm of pure movement,
the most mobile, changeable and polymorphous of all spaces" (10). On
a sea journey, the ingenuity and wily strategies of the navigators are
therefore especially called into play.

Kofman goes on to point out that there is an analogy between the *poros* of the sea journey and the strategic navigation of an "ocean of discourse" (11) by the participants in Plato's dialogues. The analogy is made explicit by Plato himself, who includes the mythological Poros in the *Symposium* in order to explain the birth of Eros, whose energy, we also learn, drives the entire philosophical enterprise.

Eros is born when Penia, who is the child of poverty, wants also to have a child and contrives to impregnate herself by Poros while he is drunk and asleep. Her strategem succeeds, and she gives birth to Eros, who has the characteristics of both his parents. Kofman teases out the implications of these mythological patterns, arguing that Penia cannot be interpreted simply as the opposite of Poros because Penia is expedient and wily, whereas Porus is passive and without enterprise. That is, although Penia and Poros retain their given identities, in Plato's version of the story each takes on something of the characteristic behavior of the other. Penia remains what she is – the child of poverty, without resources – but she is also resourceful in finding a way out of the aporia that is frustrating her. By contrast, Poros, son of Metis, is by nature wily and ingenious, but here he is passive and unresourceful. Penia therefore cannot be identified as a figure for aporia set directly over and against *poros*, and here Kofman argues that the story forces its own aporia upon us, insofar as clear identities elude us and are replaced by perplexity. She concludes that "this is why *Aporia*, which breaks with the logic of identity, and which pertains to the logic of the intermediary, is an untranslatable term" (27). And so Kofman's conclusion is virtually identical with Derrida's claim that we do not experience "the aporia *as such*", but always as mediated. Still, how we are to be sustained and encouraged in a dialogical voyage through a trackless ocean is as yet insufficiently accounted for, and at this point the part played by Eros might steer us back to Lacan, to fill out the picture.

As I have mentioned, Kofman notes that the sea is not entirely uncharted, because there are landmarks, "points of light", as well as the recorded experiences of earlier navigators. Also, when the way seems lost, openings might unexpectedly appear, and Kofman cites an example from the *Republic* where Socrates compares the dialogical process to swimming "into mid-ocean" (12), where, he says, a dolphin might suddenly arrive as if out of nowhere – a *poros*, after all, in the trackless waste into which the dialogue has led the participants. This moment of epiphany – a dolphin in mid-ocean – is surprising, but it could not have occurred unless the journey was undertaken in the first place. And so, as Kofman concludes, we are to learn that dialogue is a voyage of discovery fraught with aporias, by means of which we might arrive, however unexpectedly and intermittently, at moments of illumination that intimate some further gratification, some fuller understanding that, in turn, is a promise of homecoming. The impulse to seek and invent stratagems for finding out directions en route is supplied then by the child of Poros and Penia – Eros, who fills us with the longing that Lacan describes as desire. And so Derrida's claim about the impossibility of the "aporia *as such*" and Lacan's about the impossibility of desire being satisfied converge. In so doing, they confirm that dialogue is the process through which we shape our lives through shared experiences of illumination and understanding, which might come to light surprisingly through our encounters with the aporetic. In turn, this process is sustained by Eros, whose power, according to Plato, underpins philosophy itself.

The connections between Eros, *poros*, and illumination can bring us now to a further important study of Plato's dialogues, overlapping with and complementing Kofman's. In *Spectacles of Truth in Classical Greek Philosophy*, Andrea Nightingale[9] argues that, for Plato, philosophy begins as a response to the surprise and wonder caused by the aporetic. In undertaking a voyage of discovery in search of a solution, the philosopher then becomes *atopos*, or homeless, as once again, Eros "compels the philosophic soul to seek and find a path towards truth". Because this search is endless, the soul enters into "a permanent state of *atopia*" (106).

In the *Republic*, Plato's cave allegory shows the connection between illumination and homelessness in an especially arresting manner. Plato describes how prisoners in an underground cave are unable to converse with one another because their heads are held in a fixed position and they see only images projected onto a wall. But one prisoner escapes and makes his way to the sunlit world above. Initially he is blinded by the light, but he soon sees a world that is more real than the world of shadows in the cave below. However, when he returns to share his discovery, he cannot see clearly in the half-light, and he appears so foolish and out of control that he is abused and attacked.

Nightingale emphasizes the connection in this story between aporia – the dead-end existence of the cave-dwellers as well as the disorientation of the returning prisoner – and the *atopia* of the philosopher who, like the prisoner, finds his way to a higher form of knowledge but discovers that he can no longer be at home in his old habitat with its shadowy illusions. In this context, Nightingale also makes a distinction between the ideal philosopher whose education is described in the *Republic* as a whole and the reader who is engaged in a philosophical search but is far from realizing the ideal (105). The complexity and diversity of argument in the *Republic* can therefore remind us that for ordinary philosophers (and readers), the way forward remains incomplete and filled with difficulties, even though there are moments of revelation and discovery – dolphins in mid-ocean – to encourage and inspire.

As I have mentioned, a further source of aporia in Plato's dialogues arises from the interplay throughout between the oral and written dimensions of language. Writing stabilizes ideas and arguments, making them available for rereading and assessment, and arguments then can be subjected to more logical rigor than can be maintained in actual, extended conversations. Simultaneously, the performative aspects of language are vividly expressed through the clash of personalities and a spontaneity of speech that continually test the conceptual by measuring it against personal experience. Plato's inexhaustible richness is partly a result of the immense fertility of the aporias that are produced at the interface between orality and literacy, as concepts contend with metaphors, ideals confront actuality, and *logos* challenges *mythos*. Yet these opposites not only stand over and against each other; they also define each other within the complex, shifting network of language as a whole, and, as ever, the dialogical process ensures that neither of the opposed domains has the final word. And so, in the *Republic*, the ideal state remains out of reach just as the philosopher-reader remains on the way, because, as Nightingale says, "unlike the perfected wise man, the human philosopher never attains full erotic or intellectual satisfaction" (116). Lacan, Derrida, and Bakhtin would agree. And yet, through the unresolved interplay among aporia, *atopia*, and epiphany, the dialogue takes on its own, endlessly incomplete, endlessly gratifying life.

Art and epiphany

Hans-Georg Gadamer, who studied Plato carefully, reminds us also that dialogue is unpredictable and unfinalizable. In addition, he emphasizes that we are already within dialogue because we are immersed in language even though we are never quite at home there. Di Cesare points out that Gadamer especially valued the "right" word – the word "that reaches the you" – because that is where "the I finds a home – a home that, however, because of the irrevocable homelessness of language, always remains fleeting". Within the perpetual *atopia*, certain moments of rightness, or "fusions of horizons", as Gadamer says, can nonetheless provide openings and insights by which we shape the values that give form and meaning to our limited self-fashioning and to the narratives of what we take ourselves to be. Di Cesare goes on to state that today, "all forms of everyday dialogue are impoverished", and ordinary discourse has increasingly taken on the "'normal' form of blaming the other", a development that in turn is "traced back to both the inability to listen and the inability to speak".[10]

The impoverishment that Di Cesare notices has been a main concern of this book insofar as I have attended to the complexities of language, in which gains acquired at earlier phases of development remain the foundation of further, emergent levels of expression and communication. It is all too easy to ignore this complexity, even though, as far as language is concerned, the conservation of gains is as important as it is in the history of physical evolution, from which, indeed, our capacity for speech cannot be separated. It follows that communication is impoverished when it does not engage with the full range of language. As Plato knew very well, ideas become convincing, transformative, when they are reconnected to the tacit layers of understanding where language is enlivened by the wellsprings of emotion. Such a reconnection comes about especially through actual face-to-face dialogue, and in written form is most effectively reproduced when the strategies of literature (metaphor, symbolism, narrative, allegory) deploy language that is moving as well as intellectually convincing. As Wolfgang Iser says, literary texts respond in complex ways to the ideas and thought systems that they present, and this response establishes a "dialogue" within the work itself.[11] Along similar lines, Maurice Merleau-Ponty argues that art provides a certain manner of interpreting the world in which individual components within the work remain in tension but are harmonized. It is as if the implicit aporias are infused with an encompassing harmony that constitutes the vision of the work as a whole, which Merleau-Ponty describes as an "emblem".[12] In such a view, art is not merely an embellishment, a "cultural" distraction from the impersonal grind of the day-to-day. Rather, it shows us how we discover truth and how we relate to each other, as it invites us also to consider why these things matter. Plato's dolphins, unexpected and magical, therefore go on appearing before us in paintings, or poems or musical performances, indicating directions and enlivening desire.

Yet it seems that an adequate imagining of the way ahead cannot dispense with the aporetic, and Plato's reader-philosopher has to make do with glimpses of the Real while continuing to deal with the shadows and illusions of everyday life, a challenge comparable to the problems at the foot of the mountain in the story of Jesus's transfiguration. As Unamuno says, radical contradiction is the only foundation for a morality that is true to the sort of creatures we are. In an analogous manner, I have been suggesting that dialogue is our best means for embodying such a morality in our relations with one another, neither surrendering desire nor evading a tragic view of life. With these points in mind, I want now to consider a literary example and two paintings as a means of restoring to the discussion some sense of the dialogical engagements through which aporias are encountered and epiphanies occur by way of the process whereby, as John Henry Newman has it, notional assent (based on reason) becomes real assent (which is personal).

Pathways: Richard Rolle and Vincent van Gogh

The English visionary Richard Rolle (c. 1300–1349) achieved considerable fame during his lifetime. His voluminous writings were widely read, and at the time he was more popular even than Chaucer. But Rolle was also a marginal figure. He left Oxford without graduating, made himself a habit from his sister's clothes, and set off to become a hermit. In his best-known work, *Incendium Amoris*,[13] he acknowledges that he is "differently ordered" from other people, and he takes exception to those who have unhelpfully "tried to make [him] conform to their pattern" (142). Finding a way ahead was not easy for him, but he was not entirely adrift or without bearings, and he was able to discover his own "pattern" to follow. The main trouble with sinners, he writes, is that "their love has no pattern" (51), and they are perpetually lost. In his own case, as we learn from *Incendium Amoris*, after wandering "from one place to another", beset by "denigrations" and anger from his many "detractors" (92), while sitting alone and at an impasse – in the grip of aporia, so to say – he suddenly became aware of a "symphony of song" within himself, so that his "meditation became a poem" infused with an "inner sweetness" (93). Several times, in a similar fashion, he describes how his thinking all at once became melodious (121, 164, 177), and this synthesis of thought and music has itself the quality of the poetry to which Rolle compares his meditation.

One enduring appeal of the *Incendium Amoris* is that Rolle's writing itself often brightens into the kind of poetry he describes. This occurs partly through the modulated rhythms of the Latin prose, which is often heavy with alliteration, providing a ground bass of weighty assertion that contains the mobile exuberance, the fugitive delight of the special moments of sweetness and song. More importantly, the repeated references to sweetness, fire, and music create a pattern that plays suggestively through many variations, as the narrative proceeds. True contemplatives, Rolle writes, "know nothing within themselves but spiritual heat, heavenly song, divine sweetness" (60), and yet, although he claims that this pattern has a general significance, his descriptions of it within *Incendium Amoris* are distinctively his own. On the one hand, the threefold pattern keeps appearing before us; on the other hand, it is developed in fluid, suggestive, and surprising ways that shift and flow as Rolle explores the variety of his emotions and states of mind. Sometimes he focuses on one or another of the three elements, and sometimes he synthesizes them so that the broad effect suggests a fuller design that is engaging at the moment, though it never stabilizes as Rolle describes his unusual personal story. The poetic or literary dimension of all this emerges especially from the interplay between a singular experience marked by setbacks and aporias, while nonetheless managing to be relevant for readers at large. Yet Rolle also warns about the dangers of reading, on the grounds that books allow too much scope to "imagination", causing us, like Plato's cave-dwellers, to live "not in the truth but in shades" (145). Even a book such as he has written is no substitute for living well and finding your own way forward. As he tells us, "I have had a soul differently ordered" (142), and yet all true seekers "hasten in the same direction" even though on "different paths" (154). And so, as with Plato's allegory of the cave and the myth of Poros and Penia, *Incendium Amoris* brings the question of aporia and epiphany to us, not through reason alone (though not without reason) but by reaching to the place where concepts are rooted in and enlivened by metaphor and story, connected to the wellsprings and desire that inform and inspire our search for significance and meaning. This process finds expression especially in the literary dimension of Rolle's writing, which, I want to claim, is fundamentally dialogical, as is the case not just with literature but with art in general. And so, for instance, the silent voices of painting are also eloquent and can throw light on the concerns now under discussion.

At the end of the previous chapter I dealt with van Gogh's letters. Now, in conclusion, I would like to consider his painting, beginning with the great work made towards the end of his life, *Wheatfield with Crows*, in which he depicts a wheat field surging with sun-bright, golden energy. The field is divided by a path running crookedly in a vertical direction, then twisting off to the right, so that we do not see where it leads. At the bottom of the painting, left and right, two further paths run horizontally. We might not realize it immediately, but our point of view places us on the path leading straight ahead through the wheat, at the point where this path crosses with the other two paths, right and left. And so we are at a crossroads, a place of choice, even though the part of the path on which we stand is not shown. In addition to the divided field and the intersecting paths, the painting contains several other strong binaries. The lowering, dark-blue and black sky hangs over the golden wheat, presenting a threatening challenge to the abundant life force of the yellow fields. The portentous crows might be flying away from us or toward us – we can't be sure. The perspective that we might expect to lead the eye away pulls us instead in the opposite direction, as the wheat field seems to surge out toward us – an effect enhanced by the brown marks across the wheat, duplicating the brown paths in the foreground and causing the eye to pull the scene out rather than follow it into the distance.

Initially, these opposites clamor for us, at the crossroads, to choose: forward or back, right or left, sky or wheat, death or life? And is that path a dead end, or does it go somewhere? The extraordinary, rough power of this confrontational masterpiece is, of course, that it presents these opposites within a single image that contains them while also allowing them to be opposites perpetually caught at a point of time that forever precludes the decision that also is insistently invited. And so the aporia endures. There is no final exit until the point at which the path itself ends, but we cannot see where that is.

Undergrowth with Two Figures was painted close in time to *Wheatfield with Crows*, and van Gogh used the same double-cube format, so that the two paintings complement each other. In a letter, he provides a description: "Then undergrowth, violet trunks of poplars which cross the landscape perpendicularly like columns. The depths of the undergrowth are blue, and under the big trunks the flowery meadow, white, pink, yellow, green, long russet grasses and flowers".[14] He attached a sketch to the letter – a quickly drawn impression of the captivating, strange painting in which two people are walking among trees in a meadow of long grass and flowers. There is a row of poplars, and perhaps also a second row, merging in a way that offers several perspective lines. The couple walk close to the center, but there is no clear path to follow as they amble through the foliage and flowers. It is not clear if they are coming toward us or going away, and the lines of trees on the right and left suggest further possible walkways. Once more, the background seems to push forward as the vitality of the underbrush forces itself on the viewer's attention. Also, we see only partway up the tree trunks, which are cut off by the top edge of the painting, an effect that concentrates our focus on the underbrush.

There are many possible roads in this meadow, but then the couple is not really going along any road at all. They have already arrived. The paths are already infused with the mystery of the surrounding life force that sustains them as well as ourselves as we contemplate the cool restfulness of the scene in which the mauves, light greens, soft yellows, and whites are vital and protective, abundant and nurturing, uncharted and welcoming, and where the transient, blossoming grasses and wildflowers are offset by the stately, enduring trees. Here, in a moment of calm, we are in an oasis away from the fevers and anxieties of the everyday. The fierce energies and confrontational oppositions of *Wheatfield with Crows* are offset now by a glimpse of some other way of being, clearing, *poros*, a sense of restfulness and harmony more readily and surprisingly at hand than we might expect.

The viewer of *Wheatfield with Crows* recognizes the aporias from which we are never free, even as these are contained by the triumphant harmony of the painting itself. By contrast, the viewer of *Undergrowth with Two Figures* catches a glimpse of something paradisal, even as the painting keeps us at a distance, looking in, mindful that we are not there yet. As Jaspers says, *Existenz* is always confronting "limit situations" and the anxieties of choice.[15] And as Buber says, the way also is "nameless", so that, as with a "most complicated whirlpool", there is "no advance and no retreat, but only utterly new reversal – the break through".[16] So it is that aporia and epiphany continue within the heart of the dialogical, reproduced mimetically in art, which remains our best, and increasingly exigent, means of learning how and why dialogue is, in turn, the art itself of being human, as Dmitri Nikulin says.

In a letter, van Gogh brings us back to the metaphor of an ocean voyage that I discussed earlier in dealing with Plato, and which, in his own way, van Gogh applies to art:

> I'll risk it, I'll push off from the shore into the open sea, you'll get a certain sombre seriousness straightaway – something mightily serious rises up from inside – one looks at the calm shore, very well, it's very pleasant – but the secret of the deep, the intimate, serious charm of the Ocean, of the artists' life – with the SOMETHING ON HIGH above it – has taken hold of you.[17]

The open sea is risky, and the voyage of discovery to unveil "the secret of the deep" is "serious", but the artist is driven by an inner impulse and an encompassing desire, with the expectation that something of value will emerge to make the venture worthwhile. And as with art, so also with dialogue.

Notes

1 *The Axial Age and its Consequences*, ed. Robert N. Bellah and Hans Joas (Cambridge, MA: Harvard University Press, 2012), p. 70.

2 Charles Taylor, *A Secular Age* (Cambridge, MA: Harvard University Press, 2007), pp. 531, 514.

3 Edith Wyschogrod, *Saints and Postmodernism. Revisioning Moral Philosophy* (Chicago: University of Chicago Press, 1990), p. xiv.

4 Taylor, *A Secular Age*, p. 535.

5 Jacques Derrida, *Aporias*, trans. Thomas Dutoit (Stanford: Stanford University Press, 1993). Page numbers are cited in the text.

6 Dasein, "there being", is Heidegger's preferred term for the human.

7 Nicholas Rescher, *Aporetics: Rational Deliberation in the Face of Inconsistency* (Pittsburgh: University of Pittsburgh Press, 2009), p. 1.

8 Sarah Kofman, "Beyond Aporia?", trans. David Macey, *Post-structuralist Classics*, ed. Andrew Benjamin (London: Routledge, 1988; first published, 1983). Page numbers are cited in the text.

9 Andrea Nightingale, *Spectacles of Truth in Classical Greek Philosophy* (Cambridge: Cambridge University Press, 2004). Page numbers are cited in the text.

10 Donatella Di Cesare, *Gadamer. A Philosophical Portrait*, trans. Niall Keane (Bloomington: Indiana University Press, 2013; first published, 2007).

11 Wolfgang Iser, *The Act of Reading: A Theory of Aesthetic Response* (Baltimore: Johns Hopkins University Press, 1978), p. 80.

12 Maurice Merleau-Ponty, *Signs*, trans. Richard C. McCleary (Evanston: Northwestern University Press, 1964; first published, 1960), pp. 53–54.

13 *Incendium Amoris*, ed. Margaret Deanesly (Manchester: Manchester University Press, 1915) is the standard Latin text. The following references are to *The Fire of Love*, trans. Clifton Wolters (Harmondsworth: Penguin Books, 1972). Page numbers are cited in the text.

14 *Vincent van Gogh – The Letters*, ed. Leo Jansen, Hans Luijten, and Nienke Bakker, 6 vols. (New York: Thames and Hudson, 2009), letter number 896.

15 Karl Jaspers, *Reason and Existenz*, trans. William Earle (Milwaukee: Marquette University Press, 1997; first published, 1935), *passim*; "Limit Situations", in Karl Jaspers, *Basic Philosophical Writings*, edited, translated, with introductions by Edith Erlich, Leonard H. Erlich, and George B. Pepper (Ohio: Ohio University Press, 1986), pp. 96 ff.

16 Martin Buber, *I and Thou*, trans. Ronald Gregor Smith (New York: Charles Scribner's Sons, 1958), pp. 55–56.

17 *Vincent van Gogh – The Letters*, number 396.

6   In conclusion

To be continued

This book began as an attempt to take stock of the fact that we are in the midst of a communications revolution that is developing so quickly that it is all but impossible to manage, or legislate, or even comprehend adequately. Never has so much information been so rapidly and widely available, and yet, also never has so much dissonance and confusion arisen from so many conflicting narratives, unfounded opinions, so much uncontextualized information, and widespread, reckless disregard for circumspect judgement. Although the sheer supply of information made available by the new technologies is impressive, communication skills have hardly kept pace. As David Bohm wrote in 1996, there is "at this very moment, a general feeling that communication is breaking down everywhere, on an unparalleled scale".[1] Since then, things have hardly improved, as is easy to see today, for instance, in a widespread and pervasive cynicism about public discourse in general. As the atomic scientists cited in Chapter 2 point out, the language of politicians is now so often eroded by coarse sentiment and oversimplification that not only does it fail to inspire confidence, but it has itself become a danger. Increasing illiteracy (in the United States, Canada, and the United Kingdom, for example) serves only to encourage the encroachments of a cultural barbarism that is fueled in turn by an insatiable consumerism and the shoddy distractions of the so-called entertainment industry to which politics are increasingly annexed.

Maryanne Wolf, who understands the problems very well, correctly insists that there is no question of turning the clock back. The communications revolution is so powerful and far-reaching that digital competence is now a necessary part of every child's education. By and large, children themselves know this, to the degree even that keeping them away from tablets and cell phones is often more difficult than inducing them to learn how to use these devices. Nonetheless, there are good reasons to ration children's screen time. Not least among these is that their reading skills otherwise will suffer, and Wolf is quite clear that in the United States there is cause for serious concern about the rate at which the decline of children's reading ability is occurring. As she points out, a modern society that is not well supplied with competent readers will quickly become dysfunctional, given that so much depends on the written word in law, government, business, and education, as well as in the countless ways in which orality is itself reshaped through literacy, as Walter Ong shows. There is now abundant evidence that reading cultivates analytical ability, patience, empathy; in turn, these qualities assist in the development of a stable and flexible frame of reference, and in an enhanced ability to communicate effectively. As with the free-enterprise system, despite the depredations of "the oligarchy of private capital" (as Einstein says),[2] the communications revolution indeed has brought momentous benefits. And yet, as ever, benefits and liabilities are produced dialectically, and the damaging aspects of every innovative technology need to be identified and managed if we are to be saved from our own inventions, however wonderful. With these points in mind, I had thought at first to make a simple and straightforward case for the value of an education that promotes good reading and perceptive criticism. But then it seemed that literacy and critical reading should not be considered only ends in themselves but also as a means for promoting and enhancing civil life within a political framework. The idea of dialogue provided a way to develop a set of positions pertinent to these matters, taken together.

Throughout, I have stressed that dialogue is more than an exchange of ideas or a contest of opinions; rather, through dialogue we engage the full range of the communication skills that have marked our evolution as a species, and no key phase of this evolution is dispensable without distorting or diminishing the complex interweave as a whole. Consequently, not to engage in dialogue is to communicate partially or to fail to communicate. Instrumental and expedient forms of discourse indeed are necessary for the conduct of a great deal that goes on in day-to-day life, but the fact remains that other people are not just objects to be dealt with instrumentally and expediently. A precondition of dialogue is, therefore, an acknowledgement of the other as a person whose presence, as Levinas says, makes a demand on us even as we hold our own practical concerns in abeyance in order to gain access to that otherness. And because the other – like the other in myself – remains beyond my understanding and control, it follows that the process of exchange and discovery is *open-ended*, as I pointed out in the brief definition provided in

Chapter 1. What then might be disclosed, whatever surprising new way of looking, whatever *poros* or epiphany might occur in and through the merging of horizons (as Gadamer says) is what I mean by thinking *creatively together*, just as the attentive holding in abeyance of self-interest is what I mean by *listening*, without which dialogue cannot begin. And so, dialogue is a response to listening, and it continues through a mutual (even if often tacit) understanding that listening remains the indispensable underpinning.

In addition to describing the basic conditions of dialogue, I have placed a high value throughout on the personal (as distinct from the individual or the collective). I have done so because dialogue implicitly acknowledges that we do not become the persons we are except through relationships, the structure of which, as Maurice Merleau-Ponty says, is that "there are never quite two of us and yet one is never alone".[3] Along similar lines, Alain Badiou describes love as a "Two scene" that enables "a positive, creative, affirmative experience of difference", in turn intimating a social order where the "held-in-common" prevails "over selfishness, the collective achievement over private self-interest".[4] The personal then is political, and in its very structure dialogue also embodies this understanding. And so in dialogue, as in society at large, the good of individual persons is the good of others returned as the good of each, a minimal condition of which is social solidarity – the international of all who bear a human countenance, as Ernst Bloch has it.

To clarify how dialogue reaches back through the layers of language, I have drawn especially on the magisterial work of Robert W. Bellah and Merlin Donald, dealing with the rich interweave, both biological and cultural, that makes up the story of *Homo sapiens*. More recent discussions of the minds of infants (Gopnik), studies of perception and thinking (Polanyi), together with the broad phenomenological enterprise as a whole, confirm how language emerges from the recesses of the physical body, first through rudimentary cries and signals, then mime and gesture, ritual, myth, and narrative and the development of second-order thinking that occurred especially during the Axial Age, as research following from Jaspers has made clear. By way of the print revolution and the development of science and secularism, instruments enabling a rapid expansion of knowledge have increasingly become available, especially at the present time. I use the word "instruments" here advisedly, because instrumental efficiency has underpinned our Faustian bargains especially since the beginning of the modern era, which has been driven so relentlessly by expedient attitudes not just to one another in our economic and political lives, but also to nature. The unsurprisingly egocentric cliché that we are destroying the planet makes a point, but the reverse is the better case. The planet has had enough, and is working up to destroying us. We had better listen.

The development of the foregoing observations from the personal to the political and to the condition of the planet itself draws our attention toward those overarching questions traditionally addressed by religion, having to do with the riddle of existence and the meaning of life. In confronting these questions, we reach the limits of what we can know, and there dialogue stops. And yet we do not relinquish a desire for understanding, wholeness, and completion, as Lacan points out. Rather, we live within the unresolvable contradiction between the inevitability of the death event and our desire for life – a contradiction out of which a tragic sense emerges, as Unamuno explains. The problem of pain, the scandal of suffering, the fears and anxieties from which we are never entirely free spring up from within the gap between body and language that engenders desire in the first place, together with an awareness of the aporia that nonetheless we keep attempting to bridge. Derrida's "non passive endurance of the aporia" describes an enabling attitude in face of the unresolvable contradictions that frame our limited self-understanding, and is what I mean also by the open-endedness of dialogue urging us to remain "on the side of the sunflowers".

Derrida maintains also that the aporia is never experienced "as such", entirely unmediated, and in the gap between the tragic sense of life and the fact that we are for the moment preserved from "the worst" (as Edgar says in *King Lear*), we might best stand on the side of Nietzsche's tragic joy, van Gogh's sunflowers, Derrida's "non-passive" engagement. Insofar as the world's major religions have not careened in an all too familiar manner into reproducing the terrors and oppressions that they claim to stand against, they can also provide symbols, practices, attitudes, and aspirations that are life-affirming and sustaining in the face of life's tragic dimension and the encompassing aporia.

The value that I attach to dialogue therefore remains based on an acknowledgement that certain core contradictions are unresolvable, that we seek understandings and relationships that are not fully attainable – just as dialogue itself is unfinalizable – that we do not surrender desire even though it cannot finally be gratified, that we accept a tragic view of life even as we resist nihilism, that moments of beauty and insight are sustaining, each one a wellspring, a *poros* that opens upon fuller understanding. Following Bakhtin and Gadamer I argue that art is dialogical and, consequently, that discussions of literature are an effective way to show how dialogue works, especially in a book such as this, weighted as it is toward the theoretical. And so here we return to the concern that reading skills, which enhance empathy and analytical ability while connecting us to the deeper sources and functions of language, are at risk from the intensified instrumentalizing and fragmenting of discourse so widely in evidence today. The antidote is not just dialogue as a personal practice but a renovated education that is part of a transformation within the social order itself, of which dialogue is the symbol and art the example.

Notes

1 David Bohm, *On Dialogue* (Oxford: Routledge, 2004; first published, 1996), p. 1.
2 Albert Einstein, "Why Socialism?", *Monthly Review*, May, 1949.
3 Maurice Merleau-Ponty, "Studies in the Literary Use of Language", in *In Praise of Philosophy and Other Essays*, trans. John Wild, James Edie, and John O'Neill (Evanston: Northwestern University Press, 1988; first published, 1953), p. 82.
4 Alain Badiou, *In Praise of Love*, with Nicolas Truong, trans. Peter Bush (New York: The New Press, 2012; first published, 2009), pp. 29, 66, 90.

Index

Milton Keynes UK
Ingram Content Group UK Ltd.
UKHW022201260923
429450UK00023B/233